R&D Management

R&D Management

Methods Used by Federal Agencies

John G. Wirt
Arnold J. Lieberman
Roger E. Levien
The Rand Corporation

Lexington Books
D.C. Heath and Company
Lexington, Massachusetts
Toronto   London

Extracts in Appendix A are reprinted from *The Structure of Scientific Revolutions* by Thomas S. Kuhn, 2nd ed. enlarged, by permission of the University of Chicago Press, © 1962, 1970 by the University of Chicago Press. All rights reserved.

Library of Congress Cataloging in Publication Data

Wirt, John G.
    R&D management.

    Bibliography: p.
    Includes index.
    1. United States—Executive departments—Management. 2. Research—United States—Management. I. Lieberman, Arnold J., joint author. II. Levien, Roger Eli, joint author. III. Title.
JK421.W53   353   74-27510
ISBN 0-669-97642-3

Published simultaneously in Canada.

Printed in the United States of America.

International Standard Book Number: 0-669-97642-3

Library of Congress Catalog Card Number: 74-27510

Contents

List of Figures

List of Tables

Preface

This book describes R&D management methods used by selected U.S. Government agencies in 1972: the National Institutes of Health, National Science Foundation, Office of Naval Research, Department of Agriculture, National Institute of Mental Health, Office of Economic Opportunity, Goddard Space Flight Center of NASA, and the Air Force.

The selection provides wide coverage of the R&D management methods used by federal agencies, but does not cover all agencies that manage R&D nor all the methods used by the agencies selected. Rather, the book describes only some of the best developed and most distinctive practices, and for that reason should be regarded only as a selective, state-of-the-art review of federal R&D management practices.

A unique approach is taken in describing each agency's R&D management method. First, a conceptual framework is developed that decomposes the R&D management process in federal agencies into a number of constituent categories of activities. Then each agency's R&D management method is described by presenting the activities it conducts within each category. The resulting descriptions can consequently be read in two ways: either (1) by category across all agencies, or (2) by agency including all categories. Reading in the first way, the descriptions constitute a range of alternatives for performing each category of activity in the R&D management process. Reading in the second way, the descriptions amount to idealized "case studies" of the individual agencies that when read in sequence, reveal fundamental differences among the agencies' R&D support strategies that would otherwise be difficult to convey in words.

This study was completed with support from the Office of Research and Development Planning (ORDP) in the Department of Health, Education, and Welfare, and is one of a series of studies in R&D management that Rand has conducted for ORDP since early 1972. Initial support was also provided during 1971 by the National Institute of Education Planning Unit in the Office of Education, as part of an effort to plan for the establishment of the National Institute of Education (NIE).

Acknowledgments

We are indebted to the many managers and staff in federal agencies and elsewhere who contributed information during the preparation of this book. Their willingness to grant interviews to discuss R&D management and organization was always generous, and their knowledge of the subject matter extensive.

The responsibility for the content of this report, however, is entirely ours. Those we interviewed may disagree with our interpretation of their statements or the emphases that we have selected in making our presentation.

We wish to extend our gratitude to Richard A. Rettig, who read and commented on an earlier draft of the report; and to Louis Carrese, William Consolazio, Howard Davis, Leon Ellwein, Edward Flynn, Thomas K. Glennan, Wayne Gruner, Stephen King, Thomas Malone, Lawson McKenzie, Betty Pickett, Senta Raizen, Lillian Reggelson, John Robins, Stephen Schiaffino, Jefferey Schiller, Saleem Shah, John Sherman, and Louis Weinckowski, who read and commented on earlier drafts of portions of this book.

A special debt of gratitude is owed to Karen Brown, Nancy Davis, and Shirley Lithgow of the Rand staff: to Karen for converting our unwieldy first draft into a readable form; to Nancy for tirelessly typing our scribbled drafts and corrections; and to Shirley for typing our figures and tables.

The work upon which this publication is based was performed pursuant to Contract No. HEW-OS-72-88 with the Department of Health, Education, and Welfare.

Introduction

Background

The rapid development of science and technology over the last few decades and the increased social awareness of the effects on society have focused critical attention to aspects of the federal institutions supporting this growth that had previously been ignored. Society is more concerned than in the past with the governance of these institutions, with knowing how they function, and with obtaining maximum return from the public investment in science and technology.

One result of this attention has been the growth of research studies of these national institutions and their policies. These studies have followed a number of approaches. One is to investigate the formal organization of these institutions including the division of responsibility, distribution of funding, and the quantities and distribution of R&D manpower supported. A second has been to study the politics of science and technology and the processes by which policy is formulated. A third approach has been to investigate the means by which these institutions assess and forecast the effects of science and technology on society and to propose new methods. A fourth has been research on the productivity of R&D expenditures and the proper allocation of R&D resources for maximum return. A fifth approach, and the one we are concerned with in this report, has been study of strategies for operational management of R&D programs.

Purpose of This Report

More specifically, our concern will be with *describing* how federal agencies are managing "extramural R&D," which is defined as R&D paid for by the federal government but performed by nonfederal institutions. R&D paid for by the federal government and performed in federal laboratories is called "intramural R&D."

Much has been written on policies for managing R&D in industrial laboratories, but not much of it pertains to the management of extramural R&D in federal agencies because industrial R&D is more akin to intramural R&D. There is a literature on the management of extramural R&D in defense and space agencies; however, very little study has been made of the techniques and policies for managing R&D in other problem areas that concern the federal government. Because of the large expenditures by nondefense or space-oriented federal agencies and the wide variety of ways that these expenditures can be managed, this is a serious gap.

The lack of study of ways to manage R&D in domestic federal agencies became evident during the recent effort to prepare a preliminary plan for the National Institute of Education (NIE),[1] a new federal agency created to lead the nation's R&D effort in the field of education. One of the objectives of that planning effort was to prepare an organization and management plan for the NIE, but little useful information about how agencies were currently managing R&D could be found. Even less information could be obtained regarding the relative advantages and disadvantages of different R&D management methods.

Descriptive Approach

We discovered, however, that experienced federal managers have acquired considerable knowledge about how to manage R&D within federal agencies. The procedures currently used by these agencies are the result of an evolutionary, trial-and-error process, and therefore represent an accumulation of knowledge about how R&D should be managed. In this book we record some of this knowledge by describing the actual practices followed by selected federal R&D agencies.

Our descriptions of the management methods include only the essential steps in an agency's R&D management process; administrative detail and other activities common to all methods are omitted. A complete, detailed description would place an unnecessary burden on the reader, and would obscure those procedures that have the most significant effect on R&D content.

In actual practice, agencies do not follow a single management method uniformly throughout the agency or even in one part of an agency over an extended period of time. Rather, at any time, different units of an agency use various methods, and methods used in any one unit continually change. Some of the reasons for this variability are the changeable character of an R&D program as progress is made, differences in the preferences of R&D managers coupled with usual manager turnover, and the lack of certainty about the appropriate management techniques to use in different circumstances.

The methods used throughout a particular agency tend to evolve in a parallel manner, however, because of convergent forces within the agency, such as tradition and uniform management policies, which are imposed for reasons of efficiency, accountability, and control. The basic similarity of the management practices of an agency makes it reasonable to present them as representative models in this report.

If there is no single, overall management method in an agency, an obvious question is, Which of the many methods observed will serve as the prototype for specifying the management model? Our answer is that the prototype we have described is a synthesis of the most advanced features of all the variations of the basic method used by the agency. Thus, *a management method, as described here, is an idealization of agency management practices* in the sense that no single organizational unit uses, or may have used, all features of the method simultaneously. Furthermore, many of the features may not have been used continuously over a long period of time. The methods are not idealized, however, to the extent that all the innovations ever attempted by an agency are included. We do not discuss a management innovation as part of a method unless it has been used long enough to prove its feasibility and effectiveness to agency managers.

The data used to describe the management methods were obtained by interviewing federal R&D managers and others recommended by them. Approximately half of the people interviewed were program managers; the other half were supervisory and staff personnel. Seventy-six managers were interviewed, many on repeated occasions. In addition, some data from the academic literature and from agency documents were used.

Types of R&D Activities

The management methods described in this report and the agencies in which they are used are listed in Table I-1. The methods are categorized according to three types of R&D activity: fundamental research, practice-oriented R&D, and programmatic R&D; the methods listed under each type of R&D have the greatest number of features in common.

Fundamental Research

Fundamental research can be described briefly as activity undertaken to add to the store of knowledge about basic processes. The objective of this activity is to draw conclusions about natural occurrences that have the universality and permanence of laws. The acceptance of these conclusions is based on the agreement that the scientific community finds between the consequences predicted by the laws and the observed facts.

Fundamental research can be distinguished from other types of R&D activity by the way in which it is conducted. This process has been characterized by Kuhn, who calls it "puzzle-solving."[2] Kuhn's model is based on the premise that scientific knowledge is encoded in the form of solved problems and that scientists formulate new problems to solve by extrapolating from this base. The extrapolation procedure is to explore problems that the existing knowledge base suggests can be solved and that, if solved, would fill important gaps. Thus, in

Table I-1

Federal Agencies Studied and Selected Methods Used in Managing R&D

Type of R&D Agency	Management Methods
Fundamental Research	
National Institutes of Health	Dual Review
National Science Foundation	Single Review; Mail Review
Office of Naval Research	"No" Review
Practice-oriented R&D	
Cooperative State Research	Experiment Stations
Service, U.S. Department	Regional Research Fund
of Agriculture	Special Research Programs
National Institute of Mental	Applied Research
Health	Coordinating Center
	Operating Center
	Services R & D
Office of Economic Opportunity	Research and Evaluation
Programmatic R&D	
NASA/Goddard Space Flight Center	Space Flight Center Method
National Cancer Institute[a]	Collaborative Research
U.S. Air Force	Weapon System Development Method

[a]The National Cancer Institute is one of the institutes of the National Institutes of Health.

fundamental research the existing knowledge base of solved problems provides the framework that scientists use to formulate new problems and to assess both the significance and the chances of solving these new problems.

A consequence of the process by which fundamental research is conducted is that the number of problem areas in which scientists are working at any time is limited compared to all the problems that might be studied. The implication of this for R&D management is that there is little need relative to other kinds of R&D activity for federal agencies to intervene in the fundamental research process to establish priorities among problem areas.

A second consequence of the process by which fundamental research is conducted, however, is that since relevance to practical problems is not a direct criterion used in choosing problems on which to work, the scientific community, left to its own internal mechanisms, on occasion may fail to distribute its activities according to their anticipated usefulness to society. This raises several important management issues: How can management determine if such misallocation of resources exists? And how can it intervene to reduce such a misallocation without disrupting the intricate process by which research is conducted? The methods presented in this report provide some alternative answers.

Practice-oriented R&D

"Practice-oriented R&D" is activity undertaken to solve problems in society with the objective of providing a useful policy or product. In this sense, practice-oriented R&D is decision- or product-oriented.

One characteristic of practice-oriented R&D is that generally there will be several different ways to solve a problem, or at least ameliorate it, but one way will be judged better than the others according to social values for and constraints on various solutions. These values can vary greatly with geographical location and time, causing different solutions to be preferred according to the time and place. Thus, practice-oriented R&D differs from fundamental research in the directness of social relevance criteria and in the lack of a single unique solution to a given problem.

Another difference is that the "puzzle-solving" activity of fundamental research is seldom possible in practice-oriented R&D, where the base of solved scientific problems is small in many problem areas important to society. Thus, in practice-oriented R&D there is often a need for federal agencies to take explicit managerial measures to focus R&D activities on selected problems.

Practice-oriented R&D activity can include three relatively distinct sub-types of activity: research, development, and evaluation. Research is conducted to determine facts or to understand the relationship between selected phenomena important to practice. Development is undertaken to construct new products, systems, or other social interventions. (An intervention might be as large and complex as a voucher system for providing educational services or as small as a guide to available classroom curricula of a particular type.) Evaluation is conducted to determine whether specific interventions are working, and if so, why and to what extent they are successful. Most practice-oriented R&D requires that a mixture of research, development, and evaluation activities be interrelated for progress to be made. This is another difference between practice-oriented R&D and fundamental research.

Programmatic R&D

In programmatic R&D, the main objective is to find a way of solving or at least ameliorating an important national problem in a relatively short period of time. In content, programmatic R&D does not differ greatly from practice-oriented R&D. The only differences are the requirement of making significant progress quickly and the criterion of selecting problems of national importance. These differences for R&D management make it necessary to select specific R&D objectives and plan a coordinated series of R&D projects in order to achieve the designated objective within time limitations.

Types of Management Activity

To facilitate the description of actual management procedures, we divide the R&D management process into three categories of activity: program planning, program management, and program evaluation. (A *program* is defined as a coherent set of interrelated projects, each separately funded.) The types of management activity included within these categories are discussed below and summarized in Table I-2.

Program Planning

Program planning includes all the actions taken to determine inter- and intra-program priorities and also to foster, detect, and formulate new program ideas. Usually this does not include determining priorities among individual R&D projects, although such fine distinctions between what is and what is not program planning cannot be made precisely. The mechanisms used for program planning differ according to the type of R&D activity conducted. For example, in programmatic R&D activities, program planning is a visible activity, involving explicit identification of research objectives and formal specification of the type of R&D to be done and the time sequence. In contrast, program planning for fundamental research is not elaborate or formalized, but rather involves qualitative consideration of research areas in which R&D activity should be stimulated, based on discussions with members of the research community.

Program Management

Program management includes managing the continual process of generating, selecting, and supporting the projects within an R&D program. As a management process, this typically involves an *iterative and continuing cycle of management activities* that can be subdivided into five stages: project generation, project selection, project monitoring, project utilization, and project evaluation. These activities are usually performed concurrently in most programs (rather than sequentially as the word "cycle" may connote). At any time, programs consist of projects that are at different phases in the cycle.

Program Evaluation

"Program evaluation" is the management activity of assessing what a program has accomplished, primarily in order to determine what changes ought to be made in three general areas: resource allocation, management practices, and organization. Program evaluation activity is similar in purpose to program

Table I-2
The R&D Management Process

Category	Activities
Program planning[a]	Determination of interprogram priorities (a continual process) Detection and incubation of new program ideas Determination of an initial program strategy and intraprogram objectives and priorities among these objectives Reassessment and readjustment of intraprogram objectives and priorities among these objectives (a continual process)
Program management	*Project generation:* creation of project concepts and preparation of proposals (in response to program objectives and results of program evaluations) *Project selection:* determination of projects to support (in response to program objectives) *Project monitoring:* technical assistance to project performers, communication of problems and results among projects, assessment of substantive progress, redirection of effort, and fiscal auditing *Project utilization:* encouragement of the use of project results *Project evaluation:* assessment of project accomplishments, recommendations for future efforts, and evaluation of project performers
Program evaluation[a]	Assessment of substantive and managerial accomplishments and deficiencies Recommendations for changes in program objectives, priorities, management, and organization

[a]Program evaluation and program planning have assessment of program objectives and priorities as common activities, indicating one major area of overlap.

planning since its objective includes determining program priorities, but is different in at least four ways: (1) program evaluation is predicated more on hindsight analysis of completed R&D activities; (2) it is necessarily an organized rather than an unstructured ad hoc process; (3) it should be conducted by staff other than those involved in day-to-day management of the program; and (4) it is conducted periodically rather than continuously.

Focus on Program Managers

Our discussions of management activities within the three major types of R&D activities—fundamental research, practice-oriented R&D, and programmatic

R&D—focus on what is done at the working level of management and only occasionally consider higher levels, such as that of agency or division directors. One reason for this choice is that management procedures at the working level have a direct impact on the actual content of R&D conducted. Another reason is that most regular management procedures can best be observed at the working level; the activities of managers at the higher levels are more ad hoc and political. Management activities at the higher levels probably also differ much less from agency to agency than do activities at the working level. Thus, attention in this report centers on what occurs managerially at the *interface between the R&D performer and program management.*

The principal actor at the program management level in most R&D agencies is the program manager,[a] a person having substantive responsibility for R&D in a specific area. Typically, program managers are responsible for project activities amounting to from one million to several tens of millions of dollars. In some programs, especially when project activities amount to only a few million dollars, program managers have no supporting staff, or they have a small staff of associate or assistant program managers who help with substantive and administrative responsibilities. In other programs, managers have a larger staff, including managerial assistants, planners, and intramural researchers. In this book we focus on the *tasks performed by the program manager.*

Program Development

The primary responsibility of the program manager is program development—an important concept in the management of R&D that is highlighted in this report. One aspect of this concept is that most R&D programs have a program theme. In health R&D, for example, a program theme might be understanding how conscious control over autonomic biological functions can be increased; in educational R&D, it might be understanding how to use job sites as a means of making education more relevant and effective.

A program's theme is the basic idea behind the program and is usually stated as a simple end/means relationship, where the end is the postulated goal of the program. At first, the theme in any program is poorly understood and there is great uncertainty; as work progresses, however, the program theme is refined and elaborated through the support of a series of projects planned and coordinated to reduce uncertainty and produce increasingly greater degrees of understanding. The program result can be either a mature body of knowledge or a workable societal intervention.

Theme development is a continuous process of hypothesizing different

---

[a]Program managers are called program directors or program officers in some agencies.

approaches to problems, pursuing these approaches until success or failure is determined, and then, if necessary, reformulating hypotheses and repeating the process. The time required until a theme reaches a mature state can be quite long—sometimes over ten years. The original theme may evolve into something quite different over time, or it may end in failure.

Program directors must engage in all three management activities to be successful at program development: (1) program planning to formulate general hypotheses and determine priorities among objectives, (2) program management to develop and execute projects that elaborate and test these hypotheses, and (3) program evaluation to provide an independent review of progress at periodic intervals and suggest new directions.

The remainder of this report examines how various R&D agencies manage the task of program development in different types of R&D activity. The report is divided into three parts, corresponding to the three major types of R&D.

Part I
Methods for Managing
Fundamental Research

1 Overview

Four different methods for managing fundamental research were selected for description. The methods and the agencies in which they are used are as follows:

Management Method	Federal Agency
Dual Review	National Institutes of Health
Single Review	National Science Foundation
Mail Review	National Science Foundation
"No" Review	Office of Naval Research

These agencies are all major supporters of fundamental research in the natural sciences and, to some extent, the social sciences.

Similarities among the Methods

The four methods share a number of similarities, particularly in contrast to the practice-oriented R&D methods presented in Part II, which are very different from each other. The methods are similar because each is a variant of the project grant system, a basic strategy used in managing R&D.

Project Grant System

The project grant system for supporting R&D emerged during World War II and grew in usage during the next two decades to become one of the federal government's primary means of supporting R&D. The system has six basic features:

Support is awarded to a university or other institution for a particular *project* to be performed by a designated investigator (or coinvestigators) for a *limited period of time* (usually less than five years). Project ideas are generated by researchers in the performer community and submitted to the agency as *unsolicited* proposals. The management procedures for *project selection are more structured and formalized* than any other stage of the management process.

The agencies rely heavily on *technical advisors in the scientific community* (rather than on internal staff or R&D users) when determining which proposed projects to fund.

During the course of a project, investigators are relatively *free to alter their plan of work,* provided that the general topic of research remains the same.

Near the end of a project, most investigators submit a proposal to continue their work. The reviews of these proposals, in which an investigator's past record of accomplishment is carefully examined, constitute an *extensive post evaluation of work accomplished.*

Program Planning

The planning strategy in all four methods is largely informal and unstructured, with the primary technique used being informal discussion among agency managers and individual scientists. Three basic purposes of program planning in fundamental research are: (1) discovering new areas of research that are emerging and that appear to have great scientific and practical potential, (2) identifying areas of research (usually called "gap areas") where the current level of activity does not match its scientific and technical importance, and (3) implementing the planning results in various ways, by encouraging the scientific community to submit project proposals in the priority areas identified.

In determining priorities among research problem areas, program managers start with the priorities implicit in the distribution of unsolicited proposals received. Planning effort is directed toward determining what marginal changes should be made in these priorities.

Relying on "proposal pressure" in this way to determine the basic allocation of resources may be the most appropriate method in fundamental research, where, as explained in Appendix A, natural processes within the research community normally concentrate proposals on priority problem areas. Without these natural processes, program managers could not rely on "proposal pressure" as a valid guide in determining program priorities.

It should be pointed out that agencies using the project grant system differ in the degree to which program managers intervene to influence research priorities. Many, if not most, agencies are opposed to any intervention into the "natural" course of science, and limit themselves to an administrative role of processing and auditing grants. All the methods discussed in Part I of this report represent an opposite view: that agency managers should be actively involved in fundamental research program planning as well as other stages of program development.

Differences among the Methods

Problem Analysis and Relevance

None of the four methods for managing fundamental research contains provisions for imposing criteria of immediate relevance to solving particular social problems on research activities. This is because the relevance of a specific project to solving a particular practical problem is usually not a criterion used in choosing among alternative fundamental research activities. In fundamental research, relevance is a criterion applicable only in the broader sense of whether a completely developed body of knowledge, to which one project may contribute only a small part, will have important implications for society.

The four methods of management utilize basically two different ways of bringing this broader relevance criterion to bear on the research conducted. In Dual Review, the scientists largely determine project selection; thus their perceptions of the relevance of the research to society strongly influence the research activities supported. In the other fundamental research methods, the program directors have final authority for project selections and, to the extent that their thinking is independent of the scientists they contact, their preferences concerning the relevance of research to society will influence the research activities supported. Some managers interviewed thought that this is a more effective way of bringing social relevance criteria to bear on fundamental research activity, especially if top management strongly conveys to program managers a sense of responsibility for broadly representing the public interest.

Proposal Review

Another difference among the management methods is the method of proposal review used. In Dual Review, a panel of scientists assigns numerical ratings to project proposals, which are then funded largely on the basis of these scores. For this reason, the panels in Dual Review have great influence in project selection. In Single Review, projects are selected by a program director with the advice of a similar scientific panel. In Mail Review, the program director also selects projects but obtains scientific advice by mail. In "No" Review, the program director contacts scientists individually to obtain their views on project selection.

Program Evaluation

None of the fundamental research management methods emphasizes program evaluation, although the Single Review and Mail Review methods include an internal review system used throughout the National Science Foundation. One reason for this is that fundamental research is difficult to evaluate; another is that program evaluation is a relatively recent concept in federal management.

Chapters 2 through 5 outline the individual methods in detail.

2 Dual Review

History

Dual Review is a method of managing fundamental research that has been developed by the National Institutes of Health (NIH). Although there are a number of methods used by the NIH, Dual Review is the most traditional and widely used. The other methods have been developed to manage programmatic and practice-oriented R&D, and to manage activities that support the fundamental research effort. This chapter is limited to a description of the Dual Review method.

The NIH evolved from a federal intramural laboratory, called the Hygienic Laboratory, which was established in the late 1880s. In a 1930 reorganization of the federal health establishment, this laboratory was renamed the National Institute of Health and made part of the Public Health Service.

The NIH's Dual Review method of managing fundamental research can be traced in origin to the Biologics Control Act of 1902, which established an advisory board of nongovernmental, scientific experts to advise the director of the Hygienic Laboratory. In the 1930 reorganization, this board was renamed the National Advisory Health Council (NAHC) and was assigned as an advisory body to the Surgeon General of the Public Health Service, an arrangement that continues today.

The Public Health Service began awarding grants to conduct research with the passage of the Chamberlain-Kahn Act of 1918. Initially, the NIH Hygienic Laboratory and the advisory board (and later, the NAHC) had no direct role in the management of these grants.

In 1937, the first research institute was added to the NIH—the National Cancer Institute. The institute was authorized to support both intramural and extramural research grants and, following the example of the relationship between the NAHC and the Public Health Service, the new institute was to have a National Cancer Advisory Council. The Council was to advise the director of the new institute and was also given authority to approve all extramural grants in cancer research before they were awarded by the institute. For the first time, an advisory body of nongovernment scientists was given the authority to approve extramural grants. Nine other institutes have been added to the NIH in subsequent years, and all have advisory councils with authority to approve extramural grants. With the passage of the Public Health Service Act in 1944, this authority was extended to the NAHC for all non-NIH, Public Health Service extramural grants.

7

In 1946, the NIH created a Research Grants Office to administer the Office of Scientific Research and Development projects transferred to the Public Health Service at the end of World War II.[1]   Within a year, NIH raised this Office to division status and called it the Division of Research Grants (DRG).   At the same time, DRG was given the responsibility of reviewing all research grant applications before approval by the various national advisory councils. These reviews were to be performed by 25 study sections within the DRG. Each study section was to consist of a number of outstanding scientists from the extramural biomedical research community, with one of the scientists serving as executive secretary. This new relationship between the DRG and the advisory councils was the second major step in the development of Dual Review.

Until recently, the DRG and its study sections have had more influence in determining which projects NIH supported than the management staff in the institutes and the institute advisory councils. In the first years after the establishment of the DRG, executive secretaries[a] rather than the institute staffs did the research programming, most often by running workshops and conferences and traveling to universities to stimulate research applications in promising areas. In the past few years, the institutes have increased their influence on the allocation of health research money by doing more research programming and by using new management methods such as R&D centers and research contracts, where the DRG's management role is minimal.

The Dual Review management method discussed later depicts the current form in which the institutes have substantial influence on the direction of their research activity.

Organization

The NIH consists of two main types of organizational units directly concerned with fundamental research: the DRG and the ten institutes (Figure 2-1). The DRG conducts the technical merit review of most extramural fundamental research proposals submitted to the NIH for funding; the institutes fund and manage approved research projects. Of the ten institutes, nine are concerned with funding research related to a particular health-problem area,[b] and the

---

[a]Soon after the establishment of study sections, the executive secretary position was filled by a full-time DRG employee.

[b]These institutes are the National Cancer Institute, National Eye Institute, National Heart and Lung Institute, National Institute of Allergy and Infectious Diseases, National Institute of Arthritis and Metabolic Diseases, National Institute of Child Health and Human Development, National Institute of Dental Research, National Institute of Environmental Sciences, and the National Institute of Neurological Diseases and Stroke.

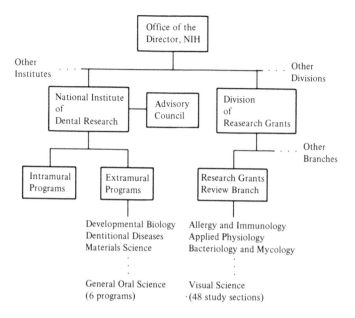

Figure 2-1. Organization of the NIH, 1972

remaining institute[c] funds projects not closely related to any of the more specific categorical areas. The smallest institute supports research projects amounting to about $10 million (FY 1971); the largest institute, about $130 million.

Most of the institutes are organized internally into an extramural research division, an intramural research division, and, if the institute supports contract research, a collaborative research (or special programs) division. Responsibility for managing an institute's extramural fundamental research activities is always assigned to the extramural division, and these divisions often operate independently of the intramural and collaborative research divisions. The institutes organize their extramural research divisions by funding instrument (the traditional way)[d] or by health-problem areas (the more recent way). Each of these problem areas constitutes a fundamental research program and

---

[c]The National Institute of General Medical Sciences. Before this institute was established, general-area research grants were funded by the DRG. These grants can be traced in origin to the projects of the Office of Scientific Research and Development that were transferred to the DRG in 1946.

[d]The instruments are research grants, training grants, and fellowships.

is managed by a *program director*. Program areas typically include research projects amounting to between $3 million and $10 million.

The second organizational component, the DRG, consists of five branches. One of these, the Research Grants Review Branch, is most pertinent to our discussion. (The other branches are the Career Development Review Branch, the Statistics and Analysis Branch, the Research Analysis and Evaluation Branch, and the Internal Operations Branch.) This branch administers 48 study sections, most of which are organized by scientific discipline. Each study section is composed of scientists from the extramural community and is managed by an executive secretary whose position is roughly equivalent in qualifications and salary to that of a program director in the institutes.

Program Development

The program development strategy used by NIH in managing fundamental research grants is essentially to rely on the scientific community to determine both the basic program ideas to be pursued and the particular projects to be performed. Project proposals, which are for the most part unsolicited, are evaluated for scientific merit by panels of extramural scientists (the study sections) in the DRG. The institutes then support, by means of a research grant, those projects judged to be of highest merit. NIH program managers affect the content of research activities supported in several ways: by stimulating project proposals in areas judged by the institutes to be relevant to their problems, or by funding selected proposals, again for relevance reasons, at higher priority than determined by the scientific panels.

In conjunction with research project grants, the NIH provides other forms of support as part of their program development strategy. These other forms are largely intended to develop the capacity of the biomedical research community and include:

Training grants to institutions for the support of graduate and undergraduate research training activities in designated problem areas.
Fellowships to selected individual graduate and undergraduate students for academic studies and research.
Research career-development awards to selected individuals for lifelong support of their research activities.
Institutional grants to selected organizations for the development and maintenance of specialized research facilities such as primate centers, or for the development of new centers of research excellence.
General (and biomedical) research support grants, which are awarded to the directors of qualifying university research departments and other nonprofit research institutions. These grants are for the directors'

discretionary use in developing research programs. The amount is determined by a formula based on the quantity of research project grants
received from NIH.

In addition, there are *program project grants* awarded to a team of several
researchers for multidisciplinary research on a biomedical problem with high
practical relevance. These grants are typically several times larger in amount
than the research grants funded with Dual Review, and they involve several
interrelated subprojects. Another form of support that NIH is beginning to
use more extensively in some institutes is *extramural contracts.* These contracts are used by program managers in the institutes to procure research
studies that are considered especially important, but for which no unsolicited
research proposals are received. Often these studies are for repetitive or special
kinds of work that complement Dual Review-funded research activities.
　　These auxiliary components of the program-development strategy are
managed with a method that is largely the same as Dual Review, except for
one important difference: a technical merit review of proposals is not performed by panels in the DRG, but by panels run by the institutes.

Management Activities

Program Planning

　　There are two sides to the planning process in the Dual Review method of
managing fundamental research grants. One is a discipline (or scientific field)
orientation of the research effort, taken by the DRG; the other is a problem
orientation, taken by the ten institutes. Neither side uses a direct method of
planning, but rather relies on indirect methods to encourage existing programs
to grow in preferred directions. Planning is limited largely to identifying
research areas that are new and becoming important, are socially or scientifically important but have been neglected, or are currently active but are yielding
limited returns.
　　The institutes use several planning modes to accomplish their objectives.
One is *internal staff work*—the program directors in an institute meet periodically as a group with their institute director to discuss institute program planning issues and the implementation of program plans. On occasion, the program directors write internal memoranda on planning issues as a contribution
to these meetings. The program directors' principal resources for these planning activities are personal contacts in the research community, attendance at
conferences, and the literature.
　　Another mode is *planning workshops.* A typical workshop format is for
a program director to arrange a two- or three-day meeting and invite a small

group of perhaps six scientists representing different aspects of a new potential research area, in addition to other scientists who might be attracted into the area. The group meets to assess the state of knowledge about the new area and to speculate on the kinds of projects that would be most promising to pursue. The purpose of conducting these workshops is to draw scientific attention to the new area and to reach agreement on priorities for immediate action. News of these priorities travels quickly through scientific circles and affects the generation and content of project proposals.

A third planning mode for the institutes is the use of *advisory councils.* Council members participate is planning in several ways: their comments on the importance of projects during their review effort may be translated into program emphases by the program directors; the institute directors may request individual council members to prepare papers on important planning issues; or the institute directors may request individual council members to participate in planning workshops. In addition, some councils have an annual policy session to discuss papers presented and issues raised throughout the year by individual members or by the institute director.

A fourth planning mode utilizes the *technical advisory committees* that have been established in some of the institutes to assist with program planning as well as other functions. Depending on the institute, these committees may or may not advise the program management staffs on technical issues and priorities, which are program planning functions; and they may or may not provide technical merit review of training and fellowship grants, technical merit review of grants for program projects and research centers, and technical advice on contract research, which are auxiliary functions. These committees meet two or three times per year.

The DRG has two planning modes. One is *workshops in discipline-oriented problem areas,* conducted in the same way as in the institutes. Another DRG planning mode is the *rearrangement of study sections,* involving the formation, combination, and discontinuation of study sections. The decision process through which study sections are rearranged is informal, largely unstructured, and internal to DRG. A number of considerations are involved, including the need to balance the proposal work load among the study sections in accordance with changes in researchers' interests, opinions of scientific leaders regarding fields that should be emphasized, and requests of high-level NIH managers (especially institute directors). The formation of a new study section for a scientific field results in greater visibility, a focal point for scientific communication, and (usually) slightly higher proposal scores for projects in the field. By administrative statute, the DRG director must review each study section's charter at least once every 10 years and decide (with approval from the Office of the Secretary) whether it should be continued, divided, or merged with another study section.

Although it is difficult to document where the greatest influence lies in the

NIH planning process—with the institutes or with the DRG—the institutes probably have more in effect. The principal reason is that the institute program directors are more deeply involved in planning activities than the DRG executive secretaries.

Program Management

Project Generation. In Dual Review, most project ideas are generated by the research community and submitted to the NIH for funding as unsolicited proposals. Some projects, however, are encouraged by institute program directors in problem areas that have been determined by planning activities to be of high priority to the institute. Various means are used to encourage submission of proposals: personal contacts in the scientific community, discussions with scientists at conferences, lectures at universities, and dissemination of pamphlets. In stimulating projects, program directors merely state areas of need, and leave the generation of detailed project ideas and designs to the research community.

To a limited extent, program directors also affect the project generation process by assisting researchers in the preparation of their project proposals. Program directors can be of considerable assistance because of their experience regarding the format and content preferred by the study sections.

Project Selection. The DRG receives project proposals three times per year. Referral officers, chosen by the director of DRG from among the executive secretaries, look through these proposals and, using a referral manual, assign each proposal to one of the 48 study sections and to one of the 10 institutes. The executive secretary of the study section receives the proposal and assigns it to one or more study section members for in-depth review. Three of these readers generally are selected for each proposal. The executive secretary also decides whether or not to form an ad hoc team to make a site visit to the principal investigator submitting the proposal. Often one of the study section members assigned to prepare a review is included on the site-visit team. These visits are made for about 15 percent of all project proposals submitted.

Following the site visits, the study section meets as a panel to evaluate proposals, with the executive secretary and one panel member acting as cochairpersons. Proposals are discussed individually for about one-half hour on the average. At the end of the deliberation on each proposal, the study section members individually vote approval or disapproval. If a majority of the members vote for approval of a particular proposal, each member then expresses his or her preference for it by assigning a score of from 1 to 5 (secret ballot). The numerical average of these scores, multiplied by 100, becomes the priority score that is assigned to the proposal. The DRG normalizes these averaged scores among the study sections and delivers each proposal to its assigned institute.[e] If a majority do not vote for approval of a particular proposal, the study section's recommendation is that the proposal should not be funded under any circumstances.

The institute program directors and staff review the proposals received, singling out those that (1) seem to have received inadequate review, (2) are disapproved by more than two study section members, (3) require funding over $100,000, or (4) are judged to be especially relevant to the institute's mission, even though they do not receive an exceptionally high priority score.

An institute's advisory council is then convened to review and approve the institute's proposals. At the council meeting, each program director discusses the package of proposals in his or her area and brings to the council's attention all the proposals that the program staff has identified for special attention. Council members review these proposals in detail. Executive secretaries also attend the meetings and, if requested to do so, interpret study section recommendations for council members. After this review, the council votes (1) to return a proposal to the same or different study section for additional review; (2) to recommend approval for funding based on the study section's priority scores; (3) to recommend approval and high-priority Rating (HPR), i.e., to change the priority score to the maximum; or (4) to recommend disapproval for funding.[f] The HPR rating is used primarily for proposals that are considered especially relevant to an institute's mission but receive a priority score of intermediate ranking. The council makes its recommendations to the institute director, who has final authority in funding decisions. The institute director cannot fund any proposals that have been disapproved by the council.

In addition to the proposals flagged by the program director, proposals may be brought up for further discussion by individual council members. Before council meetings, the institute mails to each council member summaries of all proposals to be reviewed at the next meeting, so that prior preparation is possible. Over 95 percent of the proposals considered at a council meeting are never discussed, however, because the proposal work load is so great at each session. (There are 48 study sections, but only 10 councils.) All proposals not discussed are passed "en bloc."[g]

The institutes have different ways of setting the order in which approved

---

[e]With this system of proposal review, an institute receives proposals from many study sections, and a study section grades proposals for several institutes. The actual distribution is far from uniform, however, since an institute program typically receives most of its proposals from a few study sections.

[f]The council can also vote a Low-priority Rating (LPR), i.e., provide funding only after all other approved grants have been funded, but this option is seldom exercised.

[g]"En bloc" means that all the proposals not discussed are considered as a "block," and a vote is taken to approve or disapprove the actions of the study sections regarding this "block" of proposals, without reviewing each proposal individually.

grants are funded. One method is to fund the proposals in the order of their priority score until the extramural budget is exhausted. An alternative method is to order the proposals, by priority score, within each program of the institute, and fund down to a lower score level in those programs judged to be more important to the institute. For either method, there are usually more approved grants than there is money available. The backlog of approved but unfunded grants is sometimes used in the budget process as evidence to support the need for a larger extramural research budget.

Project Monitoring. Applicants who are awarded grants receive an allotment of money to be spent over a period of five years or less, with some restrictions on salaries and equipment. Investigators are generally free to proceed without supervision, and the institutes do not closely monitor their progress; however, if the investigator finds that major changes are needed in the research approach, the institute requires that a new proposal be submitted. Minor rebudgeting among items within a grant is approved by program directors.

Project Evaluation. Most grantees propose continuation or initiation of another project after completing their original one, and the institutes process these proposals in the same way as original proposals. Accomplishments on previous projects are scrutinized by the study sections when making these evaluations, so that new proposal reviews are in part previous project evaluations. No other project evaluation mechanism is used.

Process Overview. A flow diagram of the program management process is presented in Figure 2-2.

Program Evaluation

Some institutes periodically evaluate their programs using a method called "assessment workshops," described in Appendix B. The assessment workshop method is limited in usefulness to determining the changes needed within a program; it does not apply to changes needed among programs.

Staffing

Institutes

Program Directors. With few exceptions, a program directors have M.D.'s or Ph.D.'s and generally some experience as bench scientists. Some of these directors go from intramural research to program management, but rarely in the

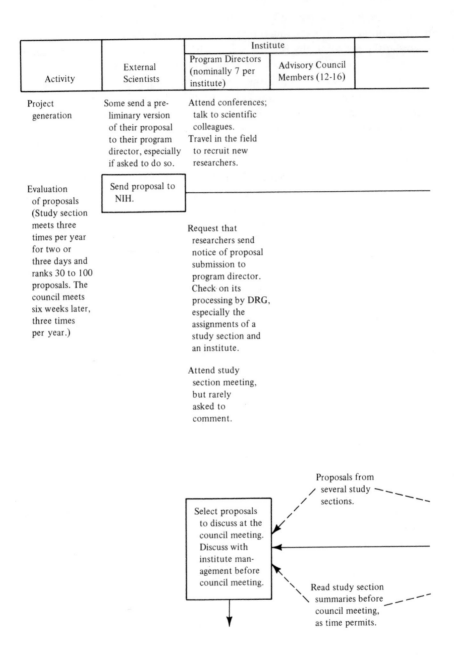

Activity	External Scientists	Institute		
		Program Directors (nominally 7 per institute)	Advisory Council Members (12-16)	
Project generation	Some send a preliminary version of their proposal to their program director, especially if asked to do so.	Attend conferences; talk to scientific colleagues. Travel in the field to recruit new researchers.		
Evaluation of proposals (Study section meets three times per year for two or three days and ranks 30 to 100 proposals. The council meets six weeks later, three times per year.)	Send proposal to NIH.	Request that researchers send notice of proposal submission to program director. Check on its processing by DRG, especially the assignments of a study section and an institute. Attend study section meeting, but rarely asked to comment.		

Proposals from several study sections.

Select proposals to discuss at the council meeting. Discuss with institute management before council meeting.

Read study section summaries before council meeting, as time permits.

Figure 2-2. Program Management in Dual Review

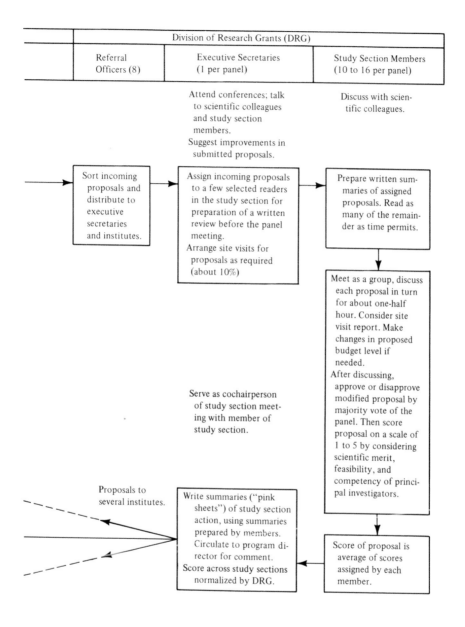

Division of Research Grants (DRG)		
Referral Officers (8)	Executive Secretaries (1 per panel)	Study Section Members (10 to 16 per panel)

Attend conferences; talk to scientific colleagues and study section members.
Suggest improvements in submitted proposals.

Discuss with scientific colleagues.

Sort incoming proposals and distribute to executive secretaries and institutes.

Assign incoming proposals to a few selected readers in the study section for preparation of a written review before the panel meeting.
Arrange site visits for proposals as required (about 10%)

Prepare written summaries of assigned proposals. Read as many of the remainder as time permits.

Meet as a group, discuss each proposal in turn for about one-half hour. Consider site visit report. Make changes in proposed budget level if needed.
After discussing, approve or disapprove modified proposal by majority vote of the panel. Then score proposal on a scale of 1 to 5 by considering scientific merit, feasibility, and competency of principal investigators.

Serve as cochairperson of study section meeting with member of study section.

Proposals to several institutes.

Write summaries ("pink sheets") of study section action, using summaries prepared by members. Circulate to program director for comment.
Score across study sections normalized by DRG.

Score of proposal is average of scores assigned by each member.

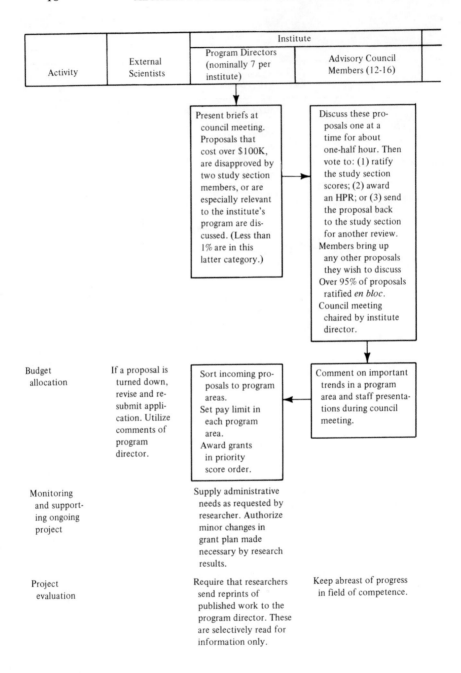

Activity	External Scientists	Institute	
		Program Directors (nominally 7 per institute)	Advisory Council Members (12-16)
		Present briefs at council meeting. Proposals that cost over $100K, are disapproved by two study section members, or are especially relevant to the institute's program are discussed. (Less than 1% are in this latter category.)	Discuss these proposals one at a time for about one-half hour. Then vote to: (1) ratify the study section scores; (2) award an HPR; or (3) send the proposal back to the study section for another review. Members bring up any other proposals they wish to discuss Over 95% of proposals ratified *en bloc.* Council meeting chaired by institute director.
Budget allocation	If a proposal is turned down, revise and re-submit application. Utilize comments of program director.	Sort incoming proposals to program areas. Set pay limit in each program area. Award grants in priority score order.	Comment on important trends in a program area and staff presentations during council meeting.
Monitoring and supporting ongoing project		Supply administrative needs as requested by researcher. Authorize minor changes in grant plan made necessary by research results.	
Project evaluation		Require that researchers send reprints of published work to the program director. These are selectively read for information only.	Keep abreast of progress in field of competence.

Figure 2-2. Program Management in Dual Review (Continued)

Division of Research Grants (DRG)		
Referral Officers (8)	Executive Secretaries (1 per panel)	Study Section Members (10 to 16 per panel)

Comment on proposals
discussed by council
when asked to do so
by a council member
or institute director.

Keep abreast of pro-
gress in field of
competence through
usual means.

reverse direction. Program directors are selected by an institute's associate director for extramural research and have responsibility for a single, extramural grants program area. Some institute program directors also have management responsibility for coordinating with intramural research activities.

Assistant Program Directors. Some program directors have a staff of one or, at most, two assistant program directors.

Advisory Council Members. At least six advisory council members are required by law to be authorities in health or science fields important to the institute's concerns. Two are ex officio representatives (generally scientists): one is required from the Department of Defense, and the other from the Veterans Administration. Of the remaining positions, numbering between six and eight for different councils, the tendency is for one or two members to be lay representatives and the remainder scientists. Advisory council members serve for four years. They are nominated by the institute director but must be approved by the federal administration, including the Secretary of the Department of Health, Education, and Welfare.

The official chairperson of each advisory council is the director of the NIH, but responsibility for chairing council sessions is delegated to institute directors.

DRG

Executive Secretaries. Qualifications, background, and terms of service of executive secretaries are similar to those of program directors. They are selected by the director of the Research Grants Review branch of DRG in consultation with institute staff and others. There is some movement from executive secretary positions to program director positions, but virtually none the other way.

Referral Officers. The director of the DRG selects executive secretaries to serve part of their time as referral officers.

Study Section Members. The executive secretary and the study section chairpersons recommend replacements for panel members from the community of scientists. These appointments are approved by the administration, up to the director of NIH. The term of office for panel members is four years. The chairpersons are chosen by the executive secretary.

Summary of Distinctive Features

The distinctive features of Dual Review, as practiced by NIH, are indicated in the following outline.

I. Organization

    A. Fundamental research activity is divided into programs in a *two-dimensional structure*: by scientific discipline within the DRG and by health-problem area within the institutes. The management of research activities is shared both by staff in the DRG and by program staff in the institutes, although different management functions are performed by each.

    B. The DRG management functions are performed by a panel of non-government, scientific peers supported by an executive secretary who is an NIH employee; the institute management functions are performed by its program directors and their assistants, all of whom are NIH employees.

II. Program Development

    A. The *development of research programs is determined largely by the scientific community,* through reliance on unsolicited proposals and panels of scientific peers to decide, in effect, which proposed projects are supported. NIH *program managers exert some influence* on the development of research programs by stimulating proposals in neglected but important areas and by modifying, with the councils, some actions of the scientific panels.

    B. No single person has responsibility and authority for developing individual research programs, because there are a number of *checks and balances* on the decisionmaking power of program managers and panel members. The primary checks are (1) that project selection and program planning, the two most emphasized management activities, are performed by separate organizations (the DRG and the institutes); and (2) that in project selection, advisory councils have statutory authority to reverse study section decisions.

III. Management Activities

    A. Program Planning
        1. Program planning is *an informal and unstructured activity* consisting of discussions among program management staff members, discussions between program management and scientists, workshops, advice from institute advisory bodies, and adjustments in the organization of the technical review panels. The planning objective is primarily to identify and encourage interest in research areas that are emerging as scientifically or practically important, or are important but have been neglected by the scientific community.

    2. Program planning occurs simultaneously both in the institutes and in the DRG: The former is oriented toward health-problem areas; the latter, scientific disciplines.

B. Program Management

    1. Project Generation: Some projects are stimulated by program management as a means of implementing program plans, but most are generated by scientists and submitted as *unsolicited proposals.*

    2. Project Selection: Each proposal is subjected to *several types of review*: a formal review by a discipline-oriented panel of scientific peers, a formal review by an advisory council, and an informal review by program directors within the institutes. Project selection is largely determined by the first type of review, since the priority scores assigned by the study sections essentially determine the actual order of funding among proposals.

    3. Project Monitoring: Projects are not closely monitored.

    4. Project Utilization: Program management makes no direct effort to stimulate the utilization of project results.

    5. Project Evaluation: A large percentage of proposals considered are for renewal or continuation of ongoing work. Consequently, *renewal reviews* represent extensive postevaluation of work accomplished.

C. Program Evaluation

Some programs are periodically evaluated by ad hoc peer panels, using a structured review procedure.

3 Single Review

Single Review is an R&D management method used by the National Science Foundation (NSF). It differs from Dual Review in three ways: Single Review includes essentially one proposal review stage; the scientific review panels are managed by the program directors rather than by a separate organizational unit; there is no priority scoring.

History

The NSF was established in 1950 to initiate and support basic research in the sciences.[1] It was to have a director responsible for administering the agency and a National Science Board empowered to "determine the policies of the Foundation" and to delegate responsibilities to the director. In practice, the National Science Board has defined its policymaking role by retaining the responsibility for approving certain agency decisions, while authorizing the director to make other decisions. For example, the board requires that all research project proposals that are over a certain dollar amount or involve a substantial departure from established agency practices be presented to the board for review before funding. The board also examines plans for new programs and, in some instances, requires that during the initial years of a new program all research project proposals be submitted to the board for review. Unlike the NIH's advisory councils, however, the board does not approve all research grants made by the NSF, although it has the power to do so.

The first NSF director and many of the initial staff members came from the Office of Naval Research (ONR), which at the time of NSF's founding was the major source of support for fundamental research in the United States. Not surprisingly, the NSF adopted management practices similar to those used in the ONR for both its Single Review and Mail Review management methods. (See Chapter 4 for a description of Mail Review.)

Organization

At present, the NSF consists of five main directorates: Administration, Education, National and International Programs, Research Applications, and Research. The NSF's mission to support fundamental research is assigned primarily to the Research directorate. The other directorates have been added as the NSF's mission broadened.

The Research directorate is organized hierarchically into six divisions; each division has a number of sections, and each section a number of programs. Programs consist of projects in a specific field of scientific inquiry amounting to between $1 million and $3 million, and each program is headed by a program director. Examples of these fields are indicated by the programs in Figure 3-1. All other levels in the Research directorate hierarchy are organized by scientific categories as well, so that the entire structure is discipline-oriented.

A review panel of scientific peers is appointed for each program director to assist in selecting projects and in establishing program directions.

Single Review is not used in all the Research directorate programs, but is followed particularly in programs of the biology and social sciences divisions.

Program Development

The program development strategy of NSF follows the project-grant system model in that reliance is placed on the scientific community for basic program ideas and project designs; it is different, however, in that the program directors are individually responsible for developing a coherent program of activities that produce scientifically and socially important results and in that the directors have great authority to accomplish their assignment. The program director's tasks in developing a research area are as follows: (1) to identify frontiers of science that either have been neglected or are emerging as potentially important for science and society; (2) to encourage and coordinate an array of research projects to develop these frontiers; (3) to support an interrelated series of projects on important "normal science"[a] problems; and (4) to develop new R&D talent for the future.

The program directors implement this strategy by interacting strongly with the scientific community and their panels in identifying important problems and new research approaches and in stimulating needed projects. This approach is similar to that used by the institute program staff in Dual Review, but Single Review program directors can potentially have more effect because they have the primary authority for selecting projects to be supported.

Management Activities

Program Planning

The planning modes that program directors use to identify important problem areas are similar to those used by program directors in Dual Review. Program

---

[a]"Normal science" is defined by Kuhn in Appendix A as research to elaborate and refine a body of knowledge.

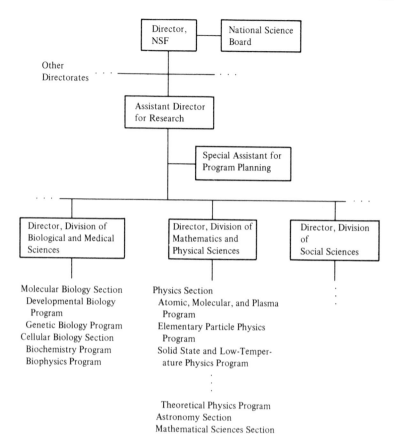

Figure 3-1. Organization of the NSF, 1972

directors talk with scientists at professional meetings and generally maintain a network of contacts in the scientific community. Program directors also travel frequently to meet with researchers or groups of researchers who are interested in important emerging areas to discuss possibilities, priorities, needs, and so forth.

A major planning difference distinguishing this method from Dual Review is that the *program directors work directly with their advisory panels in developing program plans.* They may meet periodically with the panels as a whole or talk to them individually. The panel provides the program director with advice on what is important to do, in what order it should be done, and how to do it.

The panel members also aid the program director in disseminating news of program priorities through their contacts as leaders of the scientific community.

In many instances, panelists are sought by members of this community as sources of information regarding a particular research program. The panelists are especially knowledgeable sources of information because of their close involvement in program planning and management. In contrast, program directors using Dual Review do not rely on study sections and institute advisory councils as extensively because they are not in direct, one-to-one association with these panels as are the program directors in Single Review.

Another planning mode of Single Review is provided by assigning *responsibility for research program planning to a senior staff officer,* called a Special Assistant for Program Planning, who reports (as shown in Figure 3-1) to the head of the Research directorate. This staff officer tends to specialize in finding and stimulating nascent fields of inquiry that offer great potential but do not tie in closely with existing programs. He or she uses the same planning methods as the program directors, but does not work with a permanent panel; has access to funds for sponsoring ad hoc conferences and workshops for planning purposes, but generally does not fund actual research projects; and may work with program directors, section heads, or division directors in his or her planning activities. Section heads and division directors are involved in planning activities with their program directors on a continuing basis.

Program Management

Project Generation.   As in Dual Review, project ideas are largely generated by the research community and submitted directly to a program director for consideration. (Technically, submission is made to a division in the Research directorate, but it is quickly routed to the appropriate program director.) Few of these applications are received unexpectedly, however, since most applicants contact a program director before they submit an application and present a preliminary proposal. Program directors may suggest modifications in these proposals as one means of shaping their programs. As in Dual Review, program directors may also actively solicit proposals in high-priority areas where few proposals are received. They may use the direct methods of Dual Review (personal contact, speaking tours, and pamphlet dissemination) and the indirect method of disseminating news of priorities through advisory panel contacts.

Project Selection.   At intervals of about twice per year the program director gathers together approximately 100 proposals that have been submitted since the last panel meeting or that were not discussed previously. Some are sent to members of the scientific community for mail review. Based on the review results, the program director sorts the proposals, according to personal judgment, into three categories: superior proposals that should definitely be funded, "borderline" proposals that merit consideration for funding, and low-quality proposals that do not qualify. (In some programs, all proposals are reviewed by the panel.) Typically, the "borderline" category comprises 20 to 30 proposals; the "superior" category includes enough proposals to consume a substantial portion of the available budget. Among the types of proposals generally considered to be borderline are those involving basically new ideas, ideas that appear to be outdated to the program director, or the prospective work of a new Ph.D. graduate. The borderline proposals are then sent to panel members for detailed review in preparation for a meeting of the panel to evaluate proposals. Panelists may request that other proposals that are candidates for funding be sent to them for review. Panelists are expected to submit written reviews on all proposals sent to them before the panel meeting.

At the panel meeting, the program director and panel debate the merits and demerits of each proposal selected for review. Proposals are not necessarily reviewed in any order; in some cases several will be discussed at once. Panel members do not assign a score to the proposals but give the program director their opinions and any additional information relevant to funding decisions. Occasionally the program director asks the panel, as a check on his or her judgment, to review briefly proposals identified by the program director as "clearly fundable" or "nonsupportable." Or, if the program director does not suggest this review, the panel may ask to see some or all of these proposals.

After the meeting, the program director selects the set of proposals that fits the budget and seems to offer the best balance of potential for development of new scientific frontiers, scientific advancement, and development of new research talent. Budgets of some proposals may be altered (to eliminate weak parts or to increase strong ones) through direct negotiations with the applicants. The final choices for funding are then reviewed and approved by the program director's superiors.

Some proposals also must be approved by the National Science Board. The policy that the board has established is that all projects must be submitted for review prior to the awarding of funds if they have a budget of over $500,000 for the first year or $1 million for all years, or if they represent a substantial change in policy. The board can also request that any other project be submitted for review, although this request is seldom made.

There is considerable variation in the role played by the program director in project selection among NSF programs where Single Review is used. In some programs, the panel and the program directors work as partners in the decision process, with the program director acting as decisionmaker and the panel serving in an advisory capacity. In other programs, the panel exercises much more decisionmaking authority in the selection of projects and even in determining replacements for panelists whose term of service has expired. The Single Review management method described here assumes the former situation where the program director acts as the decisionmaker; this is done to illustrate the greatest difference between this method and Dual Review, where the panel has considerable decisionmaking authority.

Project Monitoring. Grants are awarded for a fixed amount expendable over a set period of time (usually less than five years) as in Dual Review. During this time, annual progress reports are submitted, but unless major difficulties arise, the investigator is free to proceed without supervision. The program director may conduct periodic site visits to check on progress of ongoing projects, keep abreast of developments in her or his area of responsibility, and offer assistance when needed.

Project Utilization. No special efforts are made to promote dissemination and utilization of research findings, under the assumption that adequate communication channels exist in the scientific community.

Project Evaluation. Project evaluation occurs as in Dual Review: a large percentage of the projects in a program are follow-ups to previous projects; these follow-ups are subjected to the same review process as new proposals. Accordingly, project evaluation automatically occurs in proposal review.

Process Overview. A complete description of the program management process appears in Figure 3-2.

Program Evaluation

The NSF has devised an internal method for program evaluation. Division directors and the heads of the larger sections are required to prepare an annual summary of future objectives of their programs and a description of recent accomplishments. These documents are used as the basis for a briefing to the Management Council, which consists of all five assistant directors and the director of NSF. The council and managers from related programs in the NSF then ask questions about points in the briefing or other important matters.   The briefing informs the NSF leadership about the research programs and provides an opportunity for coordination among programs. These briefings also are presented in an open session for all NSF personnel.

Staffing

Program Directors

Most program directors have a Ph.D. or the equivalent and research experience. All serve full-time, but a large percentage have temporary appointments. On these appointments, program directors serve for one or two years and then return to their research environment. The other program directors serve for longer terms. Program directors are selected by their immediate supervisors.

Assistant Program Directors

Most program directors have one or two assistants who help with substantive matters and administrative duties.

Advisory Panel

Panelists are selected by the program director in consultation with his or her supervisor and are approved by higher echelons within NSF. The panelist's term of office is nominally two years, but there is no statutory requirement. Fields of inquiry are delineated so that all panelists can be specialists in a common research area, but have different experimental or methodological approaches.

National Science Board

The National Science Board is composed of 24 members; the NSF director serves as an ex officio member with full voting privileges. Members are selected because of their distinguished contributions to the basic sciences, medical science, engineering, agriculture, education, public affairs, or industry. They are appointed for six-year terms by the President of the United States with the advice and consent of the Senate.

Summary of Distinctive Features

The distinctive features of Single Review in the NSF are the following:

I. Organization

    A. The agency's total fundamental research activity is divided into a number of *discipline-oriented research programs,* each consisting of from $1 million to $3 million in projects.

    B. Each program is managed by a program director with the advice of a panel of scientific peers who are specialists in the program area.

II. Program Development

    A. *The development of research programs is strongly influenced by the scientific community* through reliance on unsolicited proposals and panels of scientific peers to provide advice on project selection.

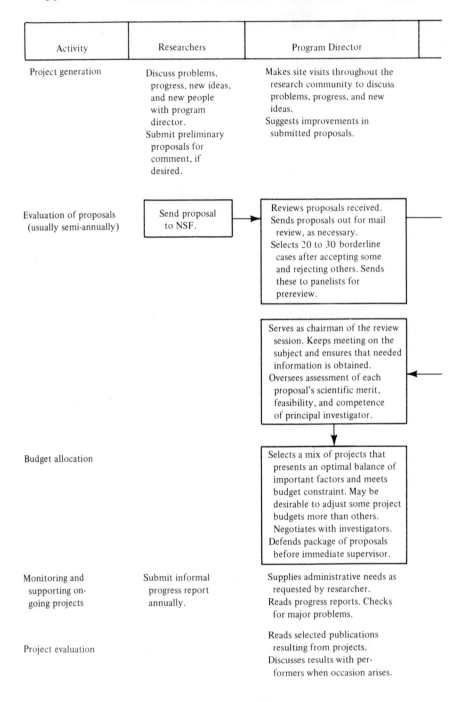

Activity	Researchers	Program Director	
Project generation	Discuss problems, progress, new ideas, and new people with program director. Submit preliminary proposals for comment, if desired.	Makes site visits throughout the research community to discuss problems, progress, and new ideas. Suggests improvements in submitted proposals.	
Evaluation of proposals (usually semi-annually)	Send proposal to NSF.	Reviews proposals received. Sends proposals out for mail review, as necessary. Selects 20 to 30 borderline cases after accepting some and rejecting others. Sends these to panelists for prereview.	
		Serves as chairman of the review session. Keeps meeting on the subject and ensures that needed information is obtained. Oversees assessment of each proposal's scientific merit, feasibility, and competence of principal investigator.	
Budget allocation		Selects a mix of projects that presents an optimal balance of important factors and meets budget constraint. May be desirable to adjust some project budgets more than others. Negotiates with investigators. Defends package of proposals before immediate supervisor.	
Monitoring and supporting on-going projects	Submit informal progress report annually.	Supplies administrative needs as requested by researcher. Reads progress reports. Checks for major problems.	
Project evaluation		Reads selected publications resulting from projects. Discusses results with performers when occasion arises.	

Figure 3-2. Program Management in Single Review Method

Advisory Panel (6 to 15 Members)	National Science Board (25 Members)

Converses with program officer
before, during, and after
review session about new
directions and program needs.
Converses with colleagues
about current research
program and prospects.

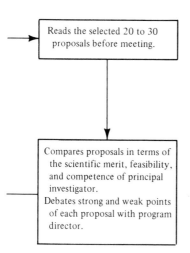

Reads the selected 20 to 30
proposals before meeting.

Compares proposals in terms of
the scientific merit, feasibility,
and competence of principal
investigator.
Debates strong and weak points
of each proposal with program
director.

Converses with program director
before, during, and after
review session.

All proposals that are for
over $500K in the first
year, $1 million in total,
or involve a departure
in policy must be reviewed
by the board.

Most proposals are renewals
of prior projects, and
progress on these prior
projects is carefully
evaluated during
proposal review.

B. *Program directors have considerable affect on the development of their programs* because of their responsibility and authority for the identification of emerging research areas, the stimulation of proposals, and the final selection of projects to support.

C. The program manager works to build a coherent and well-balanced research program in which projects are aimed at important scientific objectives, substantively interrelated, relevant to society, and beneficial for the development of a future scientific work force.

III. Management Activities

A. Program Planning
Program planning is an informal and unstructured activity consisting largely of personal interactions between program directors and the scientific community. The objective is to identify and encourage interest in research areas that are emerging as scientifically and practically important, or are important but have been neglected by the scientific community.

B. Program Management
1. Program Generation: Some projects are stimulated by program management, but most are generated by scientists and submitted as *unsolicited* proposals.
2. Project Selection: The program director has final authority for *project selection* but is strongly influenced in his or her decision-making by a panel of scientific peers.
Each *proposal is submitted to at least one type of review*—by a joint meeting of the program director and the panel, by mail review, or by the program director. Some proposals are subjected to more than one type of review. In exceptional cases, a proposal is also reviewed by the National Science Board.
3. Project Monitoring: Projects are not closely monitored.
4. Project Utilization: Program management makes no direct effort to stimulate utilization of project results.
5. Project Evaluation: A large proportion of project proposals are for renewal or continuation of ongoing work. Thus, *renewal reviews represent extensive postevaluation of work accomplished.*

C. Program Evaluation
Programs are evaluated annually through a formal but internal method of review.

4 Mail Review

A second management method used in the NSF is Mail Review.[a] This method is similar to Single Review in most respects, except that the program director uses mailed reviews to acquire all evaluative information on project proposals; scientific peer panels are used, however, for program evaluations.

Organization

The organizational structure of Mail Review in NSF is the same as that of Single Review. The total research effort is divided into discipline-oriented research programs, and a program director is assigned responsibility for each program. Related programs are combined into sections, and sections into divisions. Within any division, some programs may use Mail Review and some Single Review, although the tendency is for Mail Review to be used in the Division of Engineering and in the Division of Mathematical and Physical Sciences.

Program Development

The program development strategy of Mail Review is essentially the same in substance and perspective as that of Single Review.[b] The major difference is that in Mail Review the scientific community's influence on the program director is less direct because of the use of mailed reviews for proposal evaluation rather than direct discussion with a panel of scientific peers. Because of this difference, the program director using Mail Review has relatively more control over program development.

Management Activities

Because of the similarities between Mail Review and Single Review, this discussion of management activities is limited to the ways in which they differ.

---

[a]Much of this method is the invention of Wayne Gruner of the National Science Foundation. ·

[b]See the section entitled "Program Development" of Chapter 3.

In particular, program planning, project generation, project monitoring, project evaluation, and project utilization are virtually identical.

Program Management

In Mail Review, proposals are received by the program directors throughout the year from individual investigators. They sort through the proposals and select those that seem to qualify for funding. Each selected proposal is then sent to four or five specialists for a written review of its merits. The specialists are chosen for their knowledge of the subject area of the proposal and are given guidelines on the important criteria to consider in writing reviews. Selection of reviewers is an important aspect of Mail Review; program directors generally agree that, with experience, they learn about the biases and capabilities of the reviewers on their lists (and can, if they choose, guide the reviews obtained on a proposal in a desired direction by appropriately selecting reviewers). One of the characteristics of good program directors, however, is that they use their knowledge of reviewers to select a balanced set of readers for each proposal. Another characteristic of good program directors is that they work hard to expand and maintain their list of mail reviewers so that the best possible set of readers can be selected for each proposal. Some program directors have a list that contains almost as many names as there are researchers in their program areas.

If a proposal is complex or if it receives mixed reviews initially, additional mail reviews may be obtained. If the program director is still not satisfied, all the reviews from the first round are compiled and mailed again to all first-round reviewers, who then may choose to revise their original opinions on the basis of the reviews of others. Multiple-round reviews of this type are not uncommon in some programs.

Projects are funded whenever the program directors are convinced that it has high scientific merit and fits into their program designs. In making this decision, the program directors are motivated by the same considerations as the program directors in Single Review when they are selecting projects to fund.

Process Overview. The program management process for Mail Review is shown in Figure 4-1.

Program Evaluation

Two methods of program evaluation are used in Mail Review: one is the annual internal review described for Single Review; the other involves a panel of scientific peers specifically appointed to evaluate research programs. The panel convenes twice a year to review the projects selected and rejected and to cross-examine the program directors on their decisions. The panel evaluates all programs managed by a section (nominally six programs for NSF).

The evaluation panel session generally is not highly structured: the chairperson, elected by panel members, asks program directors, one by one, to describe briefly their decisions among the proposals within their program areas. Following presentations by all program directors, the meeting is opened for roundtable discussion. Discussion of each program proceeds until all relevant issues are considered and all opinions voiced. The panel can vote on a resolution, but usually the comments of the members are considered adequate evaluations.

These evaluations may be reflected in actual project decisions only if the program director chooses to follow them, although clear signals at the panel meetings are difficult to ignore. A program director's section head attends the panel meetings and frequently talks with the panelists on an individual basis.

Summary of Distinctive Features

Mail Review differs from Single Review in the following ways:

I. Program Management

    A. *A program director has project selection authority* and uses information and opinions submitted by mail reviewers in deciding which projects to fund.
    B. *Each proposal is subjected to review by several mail reviewers.* A process of multiple rounds of review may be used in some cases to achieve consensus on the merits of individual proposals.

II. Program Evaluation

    The program director's decisions are subject to review by a permanent panel of scientific peers appointed to evaluate programs.

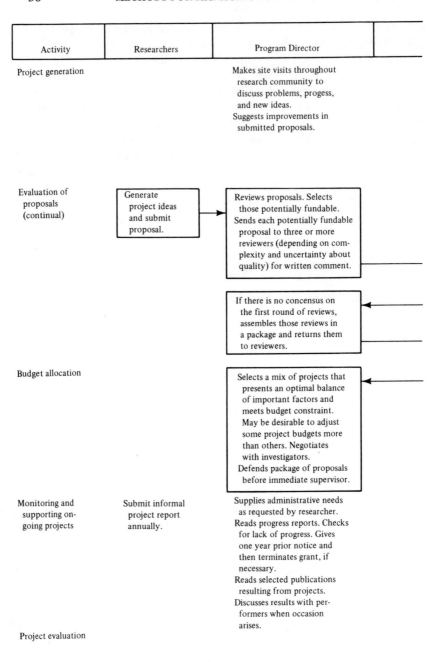

Activity	Researchers	Program Director	
Project generation		Makes site visits throughout research community to discuss problems, progess, and new ideas. Suggests improvements in submitted proposals.	
Evaluation of proposals (continual)	Generate project ideas and submit proposal.	Reviews proposals. Selects those potentially fundable. Sends each potentially fundable proposal to three or more reviewers (depending on complexity and uncertainty about quality) for written comment.	
		If there is no concensus on the first round of reviews, assembles those reviews in a package and returns them to reviewers.	
Budget allocation		Selects a mix of projects that presents an optimal balance of important factors and meets budget constraint. May be desirable to adjust some project budgets more than others. Negotiates with investigators. Defends package of proposals before immediate supervisor.	
Monitoring and supporting on-going projects	Submit informal project report annually.	Supplies administrative needs as requested by researcher. Reads progress reports. Checks for lack of progress. Gives one year prior notice and then terminates grant, if necessary. Reads selected publications resulting from projects. Discusses results with performers when occasion arises.	
Project evaluation			

Figure 4-1. Program Management in Mail Review

Mail Reviewers (3 or more per Proposal)	National Science Board

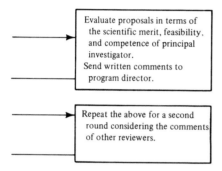

Evaluate proposals in terms of
the scientific merit, feasibility,
and competence of principal
investigator.
Send written comments to
program director.

Repeat the above for a second
round considering the comments
of other reviewers.

All proposals that are for over
$500K for the first year,
$1 million in total, or involve
a departure in policy must
be reviewed by the board.

5 "No" Review

History

"No" Review is an R&D management method that was used by the Office of Naval Research (ONR) during the years just after World War II. During the war, the Office of Scientific Research and Development and other agencies mobilized scientific manpower in support of the war effort and sponsored many projects to increase the level of scientific research applied to military problems. Dramatic results were obtained, including innovations such as radar and atomic weaponry. The results convinced many that in the future science would be much more important to national security than it had been before the war. It was also clear, however, that many of the agencies that had supported this work would be disbanded after the war, which would cause the level of support for science to return to its prewar levels. Many thought that this should not happen, and efforts were organized to establish new agencies to support science. A coalition of such forces within the Navy[1] worked for several years to develop such an agency with the department; they were able to achieve success with the passage of the Office of Naval Research Act of 1946. In the decade just after World War II, ONR became the leading government agency supporting basic research.

Program Development

Throughout the history of the ONR, and especially during its early years, some of its branches have used a distinctive program development strategy based on the project grant system. The strategy is similar to the fundamental research management methods discussed previously in several respects: Reliance is placed on the scientific community for basic program ideas, project designs, and advice on project selection; and responsibility for developing a coherent program of activities in a research area is assigned to a program director. The ONR program development strategy differs, however, in the techniques that the program directors use in carrying out their responsibilities.

One difference is that, compared to program directors who use the other fundamental research methods, ONR program directors place more emphasis on building the quality of the scientific manpower. For example, in developing a research program, ONR program directors are more willing to sacrifice

39

immediate program relevance for scientific capability than are program directors in the other methods. ONR program directors work hard to have the most capable and productive researchers in their programs. They do this by devoting much of their time to recruiting researchers of the highest quality from the scientific community.

ONR program directors also exert a great deal of effort to develop the network of scientific communications among the researchers they support by encouraging collaborative efforts, stimulating exchange of information, and sponsoring conferences and workshops. They spend much of their time developing person-to-person contacts with and among the researchers that they support. The thoroughness with which ONR program directors come to know the members of a research community is indicated by one ONR manager who said, "At the time I was at the branch level, there were probably not five people in my field not known personally to me."[2]

Although acquiring capable people and developing the network of scientific communications are important, program directors are also concerned with the substance of the research they support. They are particularly interested, as are program directors in the other methods, in detecting emerging research topics and identifying gaps in current activities so that they can determine the areas in which new researchers should be added to their programs and where communication linkages should be strengthened.

This differentiation between determining substance and acquiring people has been perhaps too sharply delineated; in reality the two orientations are difficult to separate. A program director who uses any of the fundamental research management methods does not think solely in terms of one or the other, but uses a combination of the two. The point is, however, that in the ONR method at least as much emphasis is placed on the manpower approach as on the substantive approach, whereas in the other fundamental research management methods more emphasis tends to be placed on the latter.

This dual emphasis of ONR means that less importance may be given to proposal evaluation and project selection than in the other fundamental research management methods. Program directors of ONR do not rely heavily on formal proposal review mechanisms as a means of controlling program direction. Their efforts to find highly capable researchers and attract them to the programs supplant the proposal review activities that are so prominent in the other fundamental research methods. In the words of an ONR manager, the responsibility of the program director is not to "take proposals and score them, but to develop programs."[3]

This lack of emphasis on proposal review is the reason why the method is called "No" Review. The word "No" is in quotation marks to indicate that while there is no formal review procedure, there is an informal one. The program director personally contacts members of the scientific community to obtain their evaluation of a researcher's capabilities and interests. If the evaluation is positive, the program director awards project support to the researcher. The "No" does not imply that this informal review procedure is either more or less effective than a formal one would be.

Another difference between this and the other fundamental research methods is the amount of contact that program directors have with researchers during the course of their projects. The program directors initiate site visits at least once per year, if at all possible, and make substantive suggestions. They are almost a colleague of the researchers and function essentially as a research coordinator for the projects they support.

To perform this coordinating role effectively, a program director must maintain "a really cogent grasp of his scientific or technical field."[4] He does this by talking with researchers about the substance of their research, by talking with ONR intramural researchers, and by reading and studying.

The method for managing fundamental research described in this chapter is the form of "No" Review used when the ONR was in its prime as an agency conducting research in basic science. Pressures for administrative accountability and more direct relevance to client needs have brought modifications, so that the method, as described here, is difficult to find today.

Organization

The organizational form used in "No" Review is essentially the same as that in Single Review and Mail Review in the NSF: a discipline-oriented, hierarchical division of responsibilities. Individual programs are combined into branches, and branches into divisions within the ONR. A number of intramural, naval research laboratories are also included. The organization of the ONR is shown in Figure 5-1.

Management Activities

Program Planning

Program planning in "No" Review is done qualitatively and informally as in the other fundamental research management methods. Program directors spend much of their time talking with scientists in the research community.

Program directors pay particular attention to *new doctoral graduates.* Through their network of contacts, program directors have information on the best students and their backgrounds. They arrange appointments, interview these students regarding their interests, and may informally suggest that they submit a request for support upon graduation.

Program directors arrange for *semiannual conferences,* which are attended

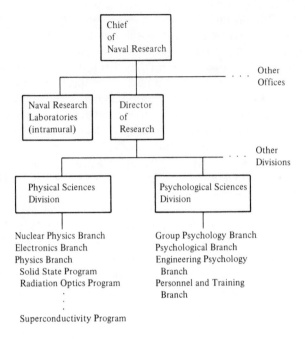

Figure 5-1. Organization of the ONR, 1969

by contractors (performers supported by the program director) and others in the same field. At these conferences, technical papers are presented and problems are discussed. Such meetings are a principal means of developing program priorities and building the social network of performers involved in the program director's field.

Another planning activity of program directors is to make frequent visits to the ONR's *intramural research laboratories* and participate in scientific staff seminars. Program directors use these sessions as a means for developing contacts in the scientific community and for maintaining their technical expertise.

One other planning technique used is that the leaders of projects supported by a program are brought in to serve as *part-* or *full-time consultants* to the program director for short periods of time. These consultants occasionally stay on as program, branch, or division directors.

Program Management

Project Generation. Because of the emphasis on building a research community by attracting quality investigators, preparation of detailed project proposals is not required. As long as the program directors have confidence in the investigator's capabilities, they are generally more willing to proceed on the basis of a tentative and brief project design than are program directors within the other management methods. Thus in the project generation stage of the management process there is more emphasis on finding investigators who will perform outstandingly in relation to program goals than on stimulating projects in specific areas.

Project Selection. Program directors usually meet with investigators to discuss their proposals. Each prospective investigator submits a proposal, but formal requirements are minimal. Proposals contain a description of the investigator's qualifications, facilities available for conducting research, a brief statement of research objectives and scientific methods to be used, and a project budget. These proposals are reviewed, but as indicated above, program directors will already have an idea of whether they want to provide support.

As the first step in reviewing proposals, the closest ONR regional office sends an officer to check on the proposing investigator's research facilities and work environment, and to discuss his or her proposal. Later, the program director reads both this report and the investigator's proposal, contacts scientists in the field to get their opinions, and may also obtain a number of mail reviews. Based on the information obtained, the program director decides whether to support the investigator and at what level. This decision is often discussed with the branch chief and with other program officers. Awards are not made at predetermined times, but as opportunities arise.

In making allocation decisions, program directors choose the projects (investigators) that contribute most to the overall development of their programs. They are expected to take a broad view of the research they support by considering its significance in relation to other fields and to society.

Project Monitoring. Each investigator supported by the program director receives one or two site visits per year. During these visits, the program director obtains information on new results that the investigator has obtained, and keeps her or him informed of the progress that others have made in the field. The program director may be able to suggest ways of solving a particular problem or at least recommend someone who can provide assistance. In performing these functions, he or she supplies an extra communication linkage that aids the total research effort.

Project Evaluation. Project awards are made for a finite period of time. At the end of a project grant, the program directors decide whether to extend the period of support. In making this decision, they contact scientists in the field regarding the quality of work that has been done and talk with the investigator about plans for the next period. Proposals are often submitted for project extension.

The program directors using "No" Review offer more likelihood of long-term support than is possible with the other fundamental research management methods. They can make this offer because of their control over project selection. With long-term support, quality of performance can be maintained, and the investigator can continue to work in a subject area of importance to the program director.

Program Evaluation

The semiannual conferences probably have some evaluation effect; however, most of the persons involved are either program managers of investigators, and this reduces the evaluative potential. In general, programs are not formally evaluated through well-defined management mechanisms, although feedback on program progress is obtained by program managers through their network of contacts in the scientific community.

Staffing

Program Directors

Most directors have Ph.D.'s or the equivalent. All serve on a full-time basis, although many are on rotation from the research community and only serve one or two years. Program directors are selected by their immediate supervisors.

Summary of Distinctive Features

The distinctive features of "No" Review, as practiced by the ONR during its early years, are the following:

I. Organization
   A. The agency's total fundamental research activity is divided into a number of discipline-oriented research programs, each consisting of between $1 million and $3 million in projects.
   B. Each program is managed by a program director.

II. Program Development
   A. *The program directors emphasize the development of a social network* within the research community supported by their programs and use this network in managing their programs.
   B. The program development strategy is to build a coherent and well-balanced research program by carefully *selecting and supporting experts* whose work interests fit integrally into the program.

III. Management Activities

    A. Program Planning

        1. Program planning is an informal and unstructured activity consisting largely of personal interactions between program directors and the scientific community. The objectives are to identify highly capable scientists who might be attracted into the program, and to identify and stimulate interest in research areas that are emerging as scientifically and practically important, or are important but have been neglected by the scientific community.

        2. An important planning technique is scheduling *semiannual conferences* of all the researchers in a program (plus others) to discuss program progress, problems, and future directions.

    B. Program Management

        1. Project Generation: *Scientists generate their own project ideas,* but program management also stimulates applications in specific research areas.

        2. Project Selection: *Program directors are almost exclusively responsible for project selection decisionmaking,* although advice is solicited from personal contacts within the academic community and from ad hoc mailed reviews. *More importance is given to the qualifications and potential of research investigators* in selecting projects than to the technical substance of the project proposals submitted.

        3. Project Monitoring: *The program director actively monitors progress on projects* by serving as a research coordinator.

        4. Project Utilization: Program managers make no direct effort to support the utilization of project results.

        5. Project Evaluation: All investigators are given support for a finite period, with the possibility of renewal. *A renewal application is evaluated as if it were an initial application,* constituting an extensive postevaluation of completed work.

    C. Program Evaluation

Programs are not formally evaluated through well-defined management mechanisms, but feedback is obtained through informal channels of communication.

Part II
Methods for Managing Practice-Oriented R&D

6 Overview

Eight different methods for managing practice-oriented R&D were selected to include here. The methods and the federal agencies in which they are used are:

Management Method	Federal Agency
Experiment Stations	
Regional Research Fund	Cooperative State Research Service (CSRS)
Special Research Programs	
Applied Research	
Coordinating Center	National Institute of Mental Health (NIMH)
Operating Center	
Services R&D	
Research and Evaluation	Office of Economic Opportunity (OEO)

These agencies are major supporters of practice-oriented R&D in different fields: the CSRS in agriculture, the NIMH in social and mental health areas, and the OEO in antipoverty programs.

Differences among the Methods

The practice-oriented R&D management methods used by CSRS, NIMH, and OEO are strikingly different. The four NIMH methods are closest to the fundamental research management methods described in Part I because they are modified versions of the project grant system. These modifications are designed to make the system more effective in managing practice-oriented R&D. The three CSRS models are based on a nationwide network of institutionally supported regional R&D centers. The form of support is a formula grant to the R&D center in an amount determined by a nonperformance-based criterion—the rural population of the center's region. The OEO method is different from either the NIMH or the CSRS methods: funding is on a project-by-project basis as in NIMH, but the problem formulation and idea generation stages of program development are performed within the agency with only refinement and testing of these basic formulations performed extramurally.

One factor contributing to the great differences among the practice-oriented

R&D agencies is that there has been practically no flow of management personnel among them, and thus very little interchange of management practices. The importance of the experience of management personnel in an agency in determining what management practices will be used is illustrated by the NIMH, which obtained most of its original management team from the NIH and uses a management method very similar to that of the NIH. Another example is the NSF, which (as was described in Chapter 3) obtained many of its managers from the ONR and adopted similar management methods.

Some other factors contributing to the differences among the agencies are that, first, their problem concerns differ, and different problems may require different R&D management methods. Second, the user communities are dissimilar. For example, the project grant system may be appropriate in mental health where there are a limited number of user institutions, but inappropriate in agriculture where the number of users to be served is much larger. Third, the R&D communities of the various practice-oriented R&D agencies do not overlap to any significant degree. R&D performers in a community exert considerable influence on an R&D agency so that it does not treat one group of performers differently from another, and this tends to reduce differences in the agency's management practices.

Similarities among the Methods

Managerial Complexity

Although there are marked differences among the practice-oriented R&D methods, there are also some important similarities. One very noticeable similarity is the high degree of *managerial complexity*. This is due largely to the combination of techniques that the three practice-oriented R&D agencies have apparently needed to cope with the difficulties of managing practice-oriented R&D.

Problem Analysis

Another similarity is the common use of *techniques for analyzing users' problems* as part of the planning process. The need to include problem analysis in the management methods is not obvious, for conceivably R&D performers could perform this function effectively. However, because all the practice-oriented R&D methods include techniques for analyzing users' problems, it can be inferred that problem analysis beyond that which would normally occur in the R&D performer community is needed in managing practice-oriented R&D.

The methods described here do not suggest, however, what is the optimal method for performing this program analysis; each agency has a different approach. In the CSRS, program analysis is performed differently: by linkage agents (extension specialists), by an appointed team of recognized scientists, or by a large task force. In the NIMH, problem analysis is performed mainly by program management staff, principally through discussions with practitioners, but frequently through groups of outside consultants or special task forces when additional guidance is needed. NIMH also supports practitioners to undertake R&D projects in their own environment, as an indirect way of performing problem analyses. In OEO, problem analysis is a research function carried out principally by an intramural policy-research staff.

R&D Priorities

A third similarity among the practice-oriented R&D methods is that all include explicit *techniques for determining and imposing priorities* on the entire R&D effort supported. The implication is that processes within the practice-oriented R&D community are generally not sufficiently selective in choosing problems, and that deliberate managerial action is needed to compensate for this. Again, different methods of setting priorities are used in each agency. In CSRS, priority setting is a complex process involving formalized and structured planning processes in two of the methods used, and interactive effects among all three methods used. In the NIMH methods, changes in priorities are developed through staff work and by discussions with review panelists and the National Advisory Mental Health Council. These priorities are implemented primarily through the actions of the review panels and the Council in accordance with their recommendations about which research projects should be supported. The staff influences the actions of both the review panels and the Council primarily through discussions with them and by stimulating quality proposals in high-priority areas. In the OEO, priorities are determined and set by performing more of the program management functions intramurally. Relying on internal staff to perform these functions and then contracting for the work to be done externally is one effective way to achieve a consensus on the R&D approach to be used and to implement that approach. This management strategy may be especially appropriate in areas such as social problems where the knowledge base is weak.

R&D Utilization

A fourth similarity, shared by many of the practice-oriented R&D management methods, is the *direct support given to the utilization of R&D results.*

In fundamental research, results are used primarily within the R&D performer community. The processes for disseminating results within that community are evidently considered adequate, because the fundamental research methods do not emphasize support for utilization. In practice-oriented R&D, however, many of the results are presumably intended for the user community, and evidently direct managerial actions are required to support the translation of these results for use by practitioners, because most of the methods include some form of support for utilization.

Chapters 7 through 13 present more detailed discussions of the individual practice-oriented R&D management methods.

7 Management Methods of the Cooperative State Research Service

History

The U.S. Department of Agriculture (USDA) began supporting research at its inception in 1862, long before most agencies supporting research today existed. At present, there are six research services in two USDA agencies supporting agriculture R&D, as illustrated in Table 7-1.

The USDA's R&D system has three major components. One is *intramural research,* which was begun in USDA's first year. Since then, it has been used as a means for developing improvements in agricultural practice and providing a scientific basis for establishing agricultural regulations. Most of the intramural research in the USDA is managed by the Agriculture Research Service (ARS), the Forest Service Research division, and the Economic Research Service. The largest of these is the ARS, which includes more than 4500 scientists in 150 laboratory locations across the country, requiring an annual expenditure of over $190 million. The largest intramural research laboratory is the Agricultural Research Center at Beltsville, Maryland.

The second major component of the USDA's present R&D system was added by the Hatch Act of 1887. This act provided for *State Agricultural Experiment Stations* (SAES) at the land grant colleges. These stations were established as a means of focusing research on the problems in each state and region and combining this research with the education function of the land grant colleges. The experiment stations receive funds from several sources: In the 1971 fiscal year, there were 53 SAESs receiving $68 million from CSRS, $25 million from other federal agencies, $210 million from state appropriations, $58 million from other local sources, and $11 million from industry. The SAESs are managed at the federal level by the CSRS.

The third component of the USDA's R&D system is the *Extension Service,* which was authorized by the Smith-Lever Act of 1914. In the early 1900s, it became apparent that simply conducting good R&D, even practice-oriented R&D, was not enough to guarantee its implementation in practice. A large effort to publish and distribute R&D results in written form had not been successful, and attempts to send researchers on lecture circuits into the farm communities had failed. The Extension Service, established at that time, has proved much more successful than previous USDA methods in increasing the rate at which new research results are adopted.

The Extension Service provides support for a small staff of professional

Table 7-1
Research Services in the U.S. Department of Agriculture

Assistant Secretary	Service
Conservation, research, and education	Agriculture Research Service; Cooperative State Research Service; Forest Service Research
Agricultural economics	Economic Research Service; Statistical Reporting Service; Farmer's Cooperative Service

men and women in each of the 3150 counties in the nation; the staff members are trained in agriculture, economics, youth work, and community development. They are known as *county agents, county extension agents, farm and home advisors.* Presently, there are about 11,000 of these agents throughout the country. They work directly with the public—individually, in informal groups, or with organizations—to help identify problems and apply the latest research findings to immediate and long-range problems, needs, and interests. When these agents encounter a problem of a technical nature or one that requires technical expertise, they consult with an *extension specialist* at the state's land grant university. While working on a problem, specialists may draw upon research that has been carried out by the SAES in their home states, the SAESs in other states, or the USDA. If there is no previous research that is applicable, the specialists consult with researchers in the SAES on possible solutions and may work with them to initiate projects to find new solutions. Also, specialists may arrange for research workers to work in the field with county agents in helping people with highly technical problems. The average number of specialists on the State Extension staffs in the land grant college is about 80.

The extension function is funded both by USDA through its Extension Service, which is part of the Conservation, Research, and Education agency, and by state and local government, which must match the federal contribution. These funds are directed to a network of *State Extension Services* located in the land grant colleges and linked to the SAESs. These State Extension Services administer the county agency program and coordinate federally initiated programmatic efforts at the county level.

Although the county agents' roles are crucial in the management of R&D, they will not be discussed further in this book except insofar as they interface with the SAES research programs. Attention is focused on the three R&D management methods used by the CSRS.

Program Development

The overall CSRS objective is to support R&D relevant to the nation's agricultural problems. Consequently, R&D activities must be supported for a very wide range of problems, including, for example, such disparate areas as agricultural production, rural life, and human nutrition. CSRS has divided its total R&D effort into 98 problem-oriented program categories. (These categories are the same as those used in USDA laboratories to classify intramural R&D activities.) Some examples are management of salinity and saline soils, appraisal of forest and range resources, control of insect pests in field crops, improvement of biological efficiency of fruit and vegetable crops, new and improved meat and dairy products, and causes and remedies for poverty among rural people. The large number of categories creates a difficulty for R&D management in the sense that developing and implementing priorities among various R&D activities becomes a difficult and complex task.

Another characteristic of agricultural R&D is that the specific problems that need to be addressed within a particular category often vary greatly with geographical location. This creates a difficulty for R&D management that CSRS has approached by creating a nationwide network of decentralized State Agricultural Experiment Stations. There is a center in every state, and several others in U.S. territories. Each SAES has the objective of conducting R&D relevant to the agricultural problems of the state in which it is located.

The CSRS has found it necessary to use three different management methods simultaneously in managing the SAESs, each with a different degree of decentralization.

The first, the *Experiment Stations method*, provides the basic support for SAESs—over 85 percent of the total funds. The Experiment Stations method is the most decentralized of the three methods used, providing CSRS with very little direct control over what projects are supported. The method does, however, provide some indirect controls; the principal one is periodic evaluation of station activities by CSRS. Each SAES receives an allotment of funds from CSRS in an amount determined by a fixed formula based on rural and farm population. The staffs of the SAESs are essentially free to generate projects and decide which will be supported with these funds. The main restriction is that in order to qualify for its share of funds, an SAES must receive at least a matching amount of funds from state appropriations. This matching requirement is intended to reinforce the incentive in each SAES to address the problems of users in the state in which it is located. On the average, states have elected to overmatch the federal contribution by a factor of 3 to 1.

The projects managed with the Experiment Station method are conducted for the same purpose as the original station activity of the first two experiment stations established in Connecticut in 1875 and North Carolina in 1877. The original purpose of these stations was to answer farmers' questions by using the latest achievements in science,[1] and this purpose has been continued in principle in every subsequent station established.

The second management method was added in 1946 when CSRS (actually, its predecessor, the Cooperative State Experiment Station Service), the station directors, and the Congress realized that the stations' R&D effort was not well coordinated on regionwide problems and not sufficiently well aligned with regard to the relative importance of various regional and national agricultural problems. The method chosen to coordinate activities was the *Regional Research Fund method,* whereby a group of researchers from the several SAESs in a region jointly plan and execute a series of projects to solve an agricultural problem important to their region. By selecting the problems that each group is assigned to solve, the station directors use the Regional Research Fund method to coordinate and to set R&D priorities in their region. The Regional Research Fund method has a priority-setting effect not only on regional research activities but also on activities supported with the Experiment Stations method, i.e., when the interest generated by regional projects stimulates station researchers supported by Experiment Stations funds to submit proposals to work in similar areas. About 15 percent of the total SAES expenditures are managed with the Regional Research Fund method, and the federal government contributes one-third of the total. In contrast to the Experiment Stations method, a state's share of federal funds is determined on a project-by-project basis. In practice, however, the total amount of funds received by each SAES for all its regional projects conforms roughly to the fixed formula.

The third management method, which will be called *Special Research Programs,*[a] provides CSRS with maximum control over R&D activities. It was added recently as a means of quickly mobilizing available research talent in the SAESs to address important nationwide problems that must be solved in a short period of time. Both the Experiment Stations method and the Regional Research Fund method have been inadequate for this task.

The program development strategy for Special Research Programs in the USDA is sequential: First, an important problem is selected to be addressed with a Special Research Program; second, a series of conferences involving station researchers (and others) is held to prepare a detailed program plan; and third, the CSRS determines the parts of the plan that will be performed by station researchers. The CSRS must obtain a special appropriation from Congress for each program undertaken. Less than 1 percent of the total SAESs expenditures is managed with the Special Research Programs method.

Organization

CSRS Organization

CSRS consists of three distinct parts: a program administration unit that manages CSRS's Experiment Station monies, a regional research coordinator who coordinates the Regional Research Fund programs, and a number of program

---

[a]CSRS actually calls these "Special Research Projects," but since a "project" consists of several subunits of activities, each of which is large enough to be considered a project, the word "programs" is substituted for "projects" here.

units that coordinate the substance of research activities in an assigned R&D program area (consisting of a number of the 98 program categories). These program units coordinate both Experiment Station research and Regional Research Fund programs. The organization of CSRS is shown in Figure 7-1.

Figure 7-1 also indicates other organizational units that are involved in managing CSRS programs, but are not formally part of CSRS. One of these units is the Experiment Station Committee on Organization and Policy of the National Association of State Universities and Land Grant Colleges. This is an organization that represents Experiment Station and land grant university interests on policy issues to the administrator of CSRS. The interests of the stations are also represented to the CSRS administrator through the Regional Associations of Station Directors, as indicated by the dashed lines in the figure. A dashed line is used because these relationships are not statutory, as between the NIH advisory councils and the National Science Board.

SAES Organization

The organization of a typical School of Agriculture is shown in Figure 7-2. It consists of several divisions: Resident Instruction, the SAES, and the State Extension Service, each headed by a director who reports to the Dean of Agriculture. The director of Resident Instruction and her or his immediate staff are responsible for the college or university program of agricultural instruction. The director of the SAES and his or her staff supervise all research activity financed by the station. Very little other agricultural research is conducted by the college or university, although some departments, such as zoology, do related research. The director of the State Extension Service and his or her staff manage the network of county agents and respond to federal extension initiatives. The extension director also coordinates the work of the extension specialists as it relates to the needs of county agents.

A School of Agriculture also contains a number of substantive departments, each headed by a department chairperson. All the professionals in a School of Agriculture report administratively to one of these department chairpersons. One distinctive feature of the organization of these departments is that most of the professionals perform two or more of three different roles: instructors in the university, researchers in the SAES, or extension specialists in the State Extension Service. To provide coordination of these multiple roles, each department chairperson reports to all three unit directors.

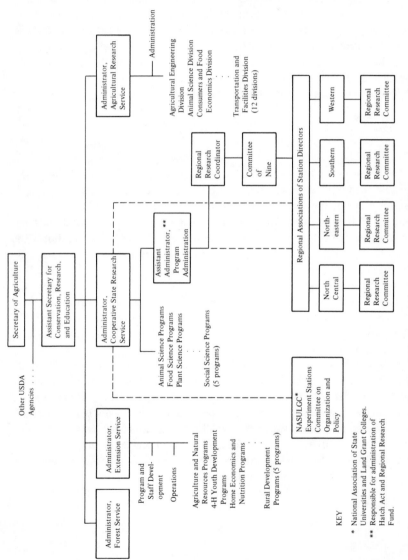

Figure 7-1. Organization of the CSRS and Regional Associations of Station Directors, 1972

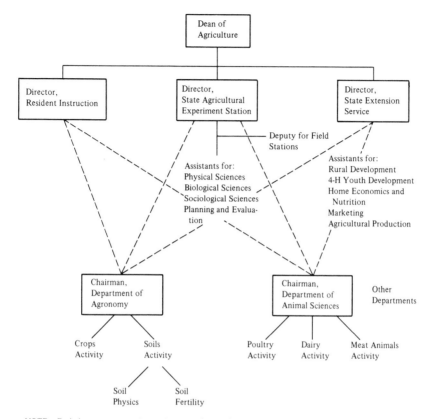

Figure 7-2. Organization of a Typical College or School of Agriculture

NOTE: Each department contains station researchers and extension specialists. Most of these personnel also teach in the university. The groupings of activity are seldom formally defined in the organizational structure.

8 Experiment Stations

Program Development

As discussed in the previous chapter, the program development strategy of the Experiment Stations method is to assign responsibility for most R&D management activities to the individual SAESs. Each SAES develops its own programs of activities to meet the agricultural needs of its home state, relying almost entirely on its research staff to generate program and project ideas and on station management to select projects to be undertaken. Because the station must meet all the agricultural needs of a state, projects are supported in almost all the 98 program categories in most stations. Although individual station researchers are free to generate their own project ideas, the researchers work in an environment that is designed to encourage working on the important agricultural problems of the state.

CSRS influences priorities in Experiment Station research primarily through periodically evaluating each Experiment Station's programs; these evaluations are conducted to influence the station director and the researchers in their choice of projects to perform.

Management Activities

Program Planning

The program planning process in the Experiment Stations method receives its basic direction from the ideas developed by station scientists at the working level rather than from the station director or other administrators. The scientists are influenced in the generation of their ideas by a number of sources.

One influence is the extension specialists who work at the same location as the scientists and ask them questions derived from agricultural practitioners' problems. In answering these questions, researchers may be guided in their future choice of problems on which to work. For particularly important questions that researchers cannot satisfactorily answer, the extension specialist may work to organize a research project in the station.

Another influence is the station directors, who may encourage researchers to change their work plans in response to research needs that the station directors may have encountered in their travels and discussions.

61

A third influence, and often the most active one, is the research program leaders. Within the departments in a station there are a number of senior researchers who function as "program leaders." These leaders, who are distinguished by their mastery of a broad field of agricultural science, may be semiofficially designated (it is written into their job description) or may have informally assumed responsibility for coordinating and shaping the research program in their area of interest. Generally, there is one program leader for about ten researchers.

Program Management

Project Generation. Project generation in the Experiment Station method follows a fairly well-defined course. As the first step in gaining approval for a project, a scientist writes up a project idea in a format called a Project Outline. The CSRS requires that a Project Outline should, in a few pages: (1) describe why the selected problem is important to the agriculture of the state and to science in general; (2) summarize previous, pertinent work on the problems; (3) state the research objectives in logical order; (4) indicate experimental methods that will be used; and (5) estimate resource requirements.

The Project Outline is a charter between the station and the proposing researcher to conduct research in a delimited area for a finite number of years (usually no more than five). At the end of this period, or sooner if changes are required, the Project Outline is either terminated or rewritten. In writing the outline, scientists consult with appropriate program leaders, department chairpersons, and the station director's office to work out a compromise that balances the interests of both the station and the researcher.

Project Selection. After the station director, the appropriate program leaders, the researcher's department head, and the researcher agree on a Project Outline, it is sent to the CSRS in Washington, D.C., for review. If the station director decides that the project should be supported with federal funds, a member of the CSRS program staff reviews the Project Outline and checks to see if the proposed work is unacceptable (e.g., mundane, ill-conceived, not clearly related to an agricultural problem, or already performed elsewhere). If the CSRS staff member decides that the proposed project is unsatisfactory, he or she can veto the Project Outline.[a] If the station director decides that the project should be supported with nonfederal funds, the CSRS staff may

---

[a]Vetoed Project Outlines, however, are usually reworked by the proposing researcher (or research team, as the case may be) and resubmitted. More than 90 percent of all Project Outlines that are vetoed are eventually approved.

read the Project Outline to keep informed on research activities, but cannot veto it.

The CSRS staff cannot veto many Project Outlines (typically, 5 percent or fewer are vetoed), because if it does, the station may fund most of the vetoed projects from its other sources and substitute other state-funded projects—effectively bypassing the CSRS veto power altogether. Actually there is no specific legal authority granting this veto power to the CSRS staff, merely the statement in the Hatch Act that the "Secretary is charged with proper administration of this Act. . . ." The understanding about veto authority reached between the CSRS and the stations is representative of the mode of operation in the agriculture R&D system. Management is viewed as a cooperative enterprise in which all parties have a voice.

Approved Project Outlines are entered into a Computerized Research Information System (CRIS) which links all the SAESs and ARS laboratories. This system provides a real-time inventory of all active agricultural R&D projects supported by federal and state monies and is used by the SAESs and ARS laboratories for planning purposes.

Project Monitoring. Once a project is accepted by CSRS, monitoring and supporting performance are the responsibility of the station staff, particularly the program leader and the department chairperson.

Project Utilization. Dissemination of R&D results is an important aspect of the Experiment Stations method, and a number of techniques are used. One is that R&D results are published in technical journals or in brochures or pamphlets put out by the State Extension Service. These publications are then distributed throughout the state through the State Extension Service network. Another way of disseminating R&D results is through the extension specialists, who are responsible for keeping abreast of progress within a certain subject area and for using new results to help practitioners solve their problems. A third way is that when a project produces results of major importance to practitioners in a state, the State Extension Service may initiate and coordinate a deliberate, statewide implementation effort.

Project Evaluation. Project results are evaluated near the expiration date of the Project Outline. A researcher's output, the need for continued research, and other factors are reviewed informally by the researcher's peers and supervisors within the station. A decision is then made to continue the Project Outline or submit a modified version. New researchers receive a more careful evaluation than researchers applying for renewal, since a decision on tenure in the department is made at the same time. Researchers with tenure are more likely to renew their Project Outline without significant change.

Process Overview. A diagram of the program management process in Experiment Stations appears in Figure 8-1.

Program Evaluation

While the CSRS is only peripherally involved in the program planning and management stages of R&D management, it does conduct evaluations of Evperiment Stations' R&D. These evaluations are based on site visits by a panel of CSRS program staff and peer scientists.

The method for conducting site visits has changed over the years, and is still evolving as the CSRS continually experiments with new techniques to solve managerial problems. Fifteen years ago, the evaluations emphasized financial investigation because CSRS program directors reviewed expenditure reports with the station directors. It was soon realized, however, that this kind of assessment was really a job for auditors and that most of the financial problems encountered could be solved with an improved project-reporting system. Accordingly, site visits were transformed from financial assessments into evaluations of current progress. This, too, was generally found to be unproductive in terms of decisions for subsequent activity. Now the site visits are used to review a station's planning process and to discuss future directions for the research programs. Most of the time is spent on the latter.

The site-visit team generally consists of one or more CSRS program staff members (sometimes including several CSRS visiting scientists) and, depending on the comprehensiveness of the review, as many as four scientists from other state stations. Reviews are conducted at a number of different levels: from an individual program-level review (the research activity in one of the 98 CSRS categories) to a comprehensive review of an entire station. Indications are that the more comprehensive reviews are more useful, although a station-level review is not considered necessary. CSRS's evaluation objective is to include the activity in all program categories in each station in at least one review every four years.

Reviews continue for one to three days. They are highly interactive working sessions in which programs are reviewed through dialogue. Typically, the first review session is a group meeting followed by discussions with individual scientists. As a means of being concrete about priorities at the program level, most of the sessions concern specific projects and their future directions.

To avoid spending too much time in reviewing the record of progress in a station's program, the CSRS program directors study the station's current and past research programs over a period of several months prior to a site visit. They obtain information on the station's research programs from the CRIS system and read final reports on research projects. Summaries of this initial study are sent to the entire site-visit team and to the station before the actual review is conducted.

Although a report on the conclusions of a site-visit review is submitted to the Experiment Station director and to CSRS, the greatest benefit of site visits is their influence on scientists in determining future research activities. Station scientists are expected to consider the content of these review meetings carefully and to integrate the results with their own research interests.

The staff of the CSRS believe that the impact of these program evaluations on the development of Experiment Stations research is as great as if CSRS were directly involved in program planning or project selection. Moreover, evaluations of Experiment Station programs also affect regional research projects and special research projects, since the station staff members are involved in all three kinds of projects.

Summary of Distinctive Features

The distinctive features of the Experiment Stations method are outlined as follows:

I. Organization

R&D is performed by a network of R&D centers, with each center serving all the agricultural R&D needs of a state.

II. Program Development

    A. Each station develops and manages its own programs of activities to meet the agricultural R&D needs of the state in which it is located. Stations support projects in almost all active CSRS program areas.

    B, The stations are supported by funds from the CSRS in an amount determined by a formula based on rural population.

    C. The CSRS's principal means of influencing program priorities in a station is periodic evaluation of station activities.

III. Management Activities

    A. Program Planning
       Program priorities in a station are determined largely by the project choices of R&D personnel, who are influenced in their decisions by information on practitioner needs relayed through a network of extension agents, the priorities of the station director, research program leaders within the stations, and the results of the CSRS evaluations.

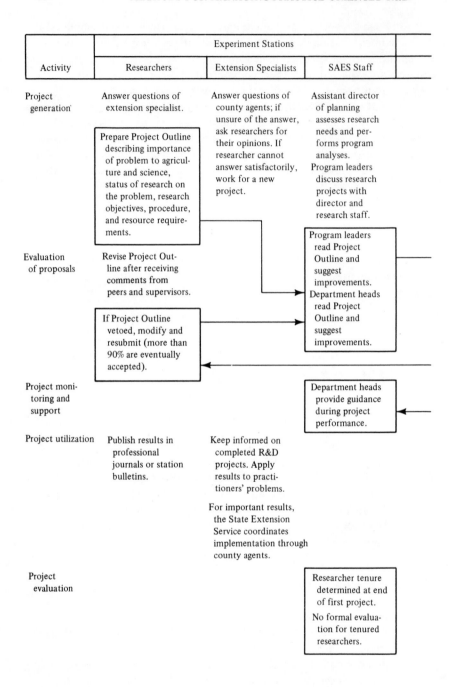

Activity	Experiment Stations		
	Researchers	Extension Specialists	SAES Staff
Project generation	Answer questions of extension specialist. Prepare Project Outline describing importance of problem to agriculture and science, status of research on the problem, research objectives, procedure, and resource requirements.	Answer questions of county agents; if unsure of the answer, ask researchers for their opinions. If researcher cannot answer satisfactorily, work for a new project.	Assistant director of planning assesses research needs and performs program analyses. Program leaders discuss research projects with director and research staff.
Evaluation of proposals	Revise Project Outline after receiving comments from peers and supervisors. If Project Outline vetoed, modify and resubmit (more than 90% are eventually accepted).		Program leaders read Project Outline and suggest improvements. Department heads read Project Outline and suggest improvements.
Project monitoring and support			Department heads provide guidance during project performance.
Project utilization	Publish results in professional journals or station bulletins.	Keep informed on completed R&D projects. Apply results to practitioners' problems. For important results, the State Extension Service coordinates implementation through county agents.	
Project evaluation			Researcher tenure determined at end of first project. No formal evaluation for tenured researchers.

Figure 8-1. Program Management in Experiment Stations

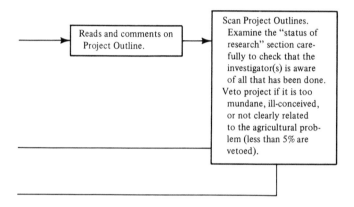

		CSRS
	SAES Director	Program Staff

Meets frequently with
statewide representatives
of agricultural interests.
Sets research objectives
and attitudes of staff
through personal
discussion.

Reads and comments on
Project Outline.

Scan Project Outlines.
Examine the "status of
research" section care-
fully to check that the
investigator(s) is aware
of all that has been done.
Veto project if it is too
mundane, ill-conceived,
or not clearly related
to the agricultural prob-
lem (less than 5% are
vetoed).

B. Program Management
    1. Project Generation: *Plans for projects (Project Outlines) are prepared by station scientists* and submitted to station management for comment and approval.
    2. Project Selection: *Each station determines the projects it will support,* subject to veto by the CSRS (a power that CSRS seldom exercises).
    3. Project Monitoring: Progress on projects is monitored by station management. No formal method is used.
    4. Project Utilization: *R&D project results are implemented by the State Extension Service,* which is an integral part of the Experiment Station complex.
    5. Project Evaluation: Each station project is reviewed by station management at its completion.
C. Program Evaluation
    The CSRS periodically evaluates the activities of each station through an on-site review conducted by an ad hoc panel of outside researchers and CSRS staff.

9 Regional Research Fund

Program Development

The Regional Research Fund method is a method by which selected scientists from a number of USDA Experiment Stations within a region plan a coordinated program of R&D projects to solve an important problem common throughout the region. These projects are actually conducted in the Experiment Stations, but planned and coordinated by a joint committee of technical experts from the participating stations. The Regional Research Fund method is also used as a means of setting R&D priorities in the Experiment Station R&D programs that address these important regional problems. The many joint discussions and efforts generated by cooperation on a Regional Research Fund program enable the participating scientists to formulate priorities for research from a regional perspective and to keep informed of other station activities. When these scientists interact with colleagues in their home stations, this regional perspective is transferred to all the stations in the region. As this broader regional outlook is reflected in proposals for formula-grant supported research in the individual stations, the priority-setting effect of Regional Research Fund programs on Experiment Station research is achieved.

Organization

A number of different organizational groups are involved in managing the Regional Research Fund programs:

Regional Associations of Station Directors from four regions—North Central, Northeastern, Southern, and Western. The Regional Associations meet triannually to manage the Regional Research Fund program and also to discuss SAES policy. The associations communicate policy decisions directly to the administrator of CSRS. Each association hires an executive director and, as needed, other regional office staff.
Regional Research Committees. There is one Regional Research Committee for each Regional Association. The Regional Research Committees assist in developing priorities for regional programs and in reviewing program plans.
Committee of Nine. This committee meets triannually to discuss policy with CSRS staff and to review projects submitted for Regional Research

Funds. Two committee members are elected by each Regional Association
of Station Directors and one by the Experiment Station Committee on
Organization and Policy of the National Association of State Universities
and Land Grant Colleges, which supports a nomination by the American
Association of Home Economists.

Administrative Advisor. Advisors provide the executive direction for
Regional Research Fund programs. They are designated by the Regional
Association of Station Directors and are recruited from the staffs of research
administrators of the state stations in the region of concern to serve for the
duration of a program. Advisors serve in their temporary assignments without changing location. While serving as advisors, they report to their respective Regional Association of Station Directors.

Technical Committees. These committees are formed ad hoc to plan each
Regional Research Fund program. The membership of Technical Committees includes one or more scientists from each cooperating state station
(appointed by the station director), a member of the CSRS program staff,
an administrative advisor, and additional consultants and representatives
of other agencies, as needed. To the extent possible, the delegates from
the state stations are the scientists who will be involved in performing the
proposed program.

Management Activities

Program Planning

Until ten years ago, the ideas and impetus for regional programs came from
the working scientists. Now the Regional Associations of Station Directors play
a primary role. Although new methods for planning regional programs are still
being explored, one pattern the Regional Associations have followed is to set
aside part of their triannual meetings for discussion of important regional issues
and to decide on one or two important regional problem areas. As a starting
point, the directors sometimes use the 32 task force reports developed during
the National Program of Research planning effort of 1966. Ideas are also
obtained from issue papers prepared by the Regional Research Committees.

The associations then appoint a *task force of department chairpersons and
leading scientists for each problem area selected.* The task force members are
selected on the basis of recognized scientific excellence and breadth of interests.
Their job is to decompose their problem area into a set of R&D objectives, each
one a candidate for a Regional Research Fund program; they also indicate priorities among the programs suggested and estimate the resources likely to be
required for each one.

At about the same time, all the station directors list their current obligations for regional research activity during the coming year and relate this information to the CSRS. The CSRS computes the difference between Regional Research Funds already committed by all the directors and the amount available from Congress, and distributes the surplus to the stations so that each has a total share roughly proportional to the fixed formula used in station research. Thus, each director knows how much of a commitment can be made to new regional research activity.

The task force's report is reviewed by the Regional Research Committee; both the report and the review are submitted to the Regional Association of Station Directors, which then considers the list of programs recommended and the available research funds and selects those programs it judges to be most important. An administrative advisor is appointed by the Association for each of the selected programs and is authorized to call the first Technical Committee meeting.

The CSRS influences the planning process by having one of its CSRS program staff members serve as a contributing member of the task force to develop candidate research programs. This staff member is highly qualified technically and helps to ensure that CSRS priorities and perspectives are brought into the planning activity.

Program Management

Project Generation. At the first meeting of a Technical Committee, the administrative advisor describes the regional research activity and the program's history and objective(s). Then, in a series of meetings, the Technical Committee identifies specific subparts of the overall problem assigned to it and ranks these subparts. Station representatives indicate their interests, and a tentative sketch of the regional program is developed. The members of the Technical Committee then return to their respective stations and discuss the plan with their colleagues.

Sometime during this first series of meetings, the Technical Committee selects a chairperson and designates one of its members or the chairperson as program coordinator. (In large programs the committee may hire a program coordinator.) The chairperson presides over the Technical Committee; the coordinator maintains contact with the researchers in a regional program through correspondence and personal visits. Frequent contact is essential to coordinate the design of experimental protocol so that findings can be easily incorporated into a regional analysis. The coordinator also reviews the gathering and analysis to assure uniform procedures.

The committee's next task, performed over a period of months, is to develop a detailed project plan (Program Outline). The Outline specifies program duration (no more than five years), objectives, organization, procedures to be used, and relationships to current and previous related work. The procedure section indicates initial plans for achieving the objective of each program subpart, methods for collecting data, schedules, and means of coordinating activity. The allocation of tasks and responsibilities among participating state stations is stated explicitly.

Each station representative must discuss with his or her station director the resources that will be committed to the program before they are included in the Program Outline. Bargaining often occurs over this matter for several reasons: The station director must allocate her or his fixed Regional Research Funds among several regional programs, and the researchers participating on each Technical Committee usually attempt to secure generous support for their individual stations. The administrative advisor, a delegate of the Regional Association of Station Directors, acts as a mediator in the bargaining process and attempts to ensure that tasks are assigned to the most competent persons.

Project Selection. Completed Program Outlines are sent to the Regional Research Committee for preliminary review and then to the Regional Association of Station Directors. Changes desired by the directors are incorporated by the Technical Committee, and revised Outlines are sent to the Committee of Nine, which is the actual legal authority for recommending approval and funding for Regional Research projects.

Incoming Program Outlines are assigned to two representatives for in-depth review: a member of the Committee of Nine and a CSRS program staff member. In writing the review, the Committee of Nine delegate may employ consultants, including CSRS personnel. At the meeting of the Committee of Nine, each proposal is discussed in turn and a recommendation is made by majority vote to approve, disapprove, or conditionally approve the proposed program. The Committee of Nine rarely disapproves a program, but frequently votes for conditional approval. For example, the committee might recommend approval for one year of funding rather than five, with the stipulation that particular issues be resolved by the end of the first year. Alternatively, the committee might eliminate parts of the Program Outline that are objectionable. In practice, the committee refuses enough proposed work to "keep the planning activity earnest." The vigor with which the Committee of Nine reviews Program Outlines varies greatly with its membership, however, a matter over which CSRS has almost no control.

Project Monitoring. Upon receiving the Committee of Nine's recommendation and CSRS approval, the state station directors initiate work on their portions of the regional program. During program performance, the administrative advisor, as delegate of the Regional Association of Station Directors, carries much responsibility for following the schedule according to the Program Outline. He or she confers with the CSRS program staff members that CSRS assigns to the program, checks on the adequacy of station participation, counsels individual researchers, and schedules at least one meeting of the Technical Committee per year to review project progress.

At these annual meetings, each participant is required to present a prepared report of project results. Committee members discuss the reports, the work planned for the subsequent year, and the desirability of changing the work schedule as written in the Program Outline. If reallocation of a particular station's resources is required, the administrative advisor negotiates the changes with the relevant station director. The Technical Committee also reviews and approves the program's annual report prepared by the Technical Committee chairperson before it is sent by the administrative advisor to CSRS.

During this phase of a program, a CSRS program staff member is assigned to each regional program to assist the administrative advisor in maintaining close personal contact with program personnel. In practice, the CSRS program staff member and the administrative advisor are the chief communication links between researchers, station directors, cooperating agencies, and the CSRS.

Project Utilization. The administrative advisor is also responsible for seeing that the Technical Committee publishes its findings widely. Station publications, journal articles, and project briefs are often used for disseminating results. Moreover, the Technical Committee must submit a final report to CSRS at the end of its funding period.

Project Evaluation. One year before the program is scheduled to end, the Technical Committee must decide whether, during the next five-year period, the program should be terminated, extended with the same Program Outline, or revised and performed under a modified Outline. The administrative advisor organizes the required meetings and assignments for carrying out whatever action must be taken. If the Program Outline is to be changed significantly, the process of developing a new Outline is not unlike the one followed in preparing the original Program Outline. In any case, requests for both extension and revision of Program Outlines must go through the same evaluation steps as initial proposals.

Process Overview. A diagram of the major program management activities appears in Figure 9-1.

Program Evaluation

Procedures for evaluating regional projects vary by region and by project. There is no uniform method of evaluating except that each project is reviewed after one or two years by the Committee of Nine. This review is based primarily on the formal report submitted by the administrative advisor, with supplementary comments from CSRS program staff members.

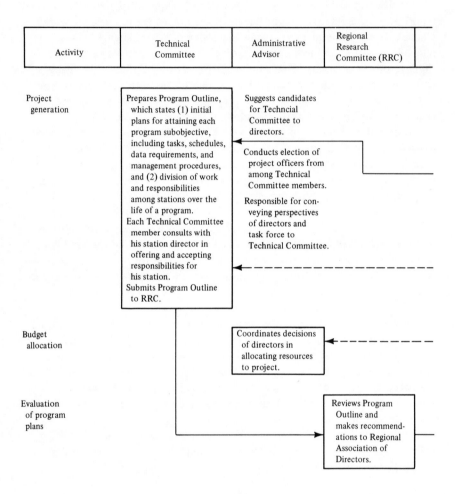

Activity	Technical Committee	Administrative Advisor	Regional Research Committee (RRC)	
Project generation	Prepares Program Outline, which states (1) initial plans for attaining each program subobjective, including tasks, schedules, data requirements, and management procedures, and (2) division of work and responsibilities among stations over the life of a program. Each Technical Committee member consults with his station director in offering and accepting responsibilities for his station. Submits Program Outline to RRC.	Suggests candidates for Techncial Committee to directors. Conducts election of project officers from among Technical Committee members. Responsible for conveying perspectives of directors and task force to Technical Committee.		
Budget allocation		Coordinates decisions of directors in allocating resources to project.		
Evaluation of program plans			Reviews Program Outline and makes recommendations to Regional Association of Directors.	

Figure 9-1. Program Management in Regional Research Fund Programs

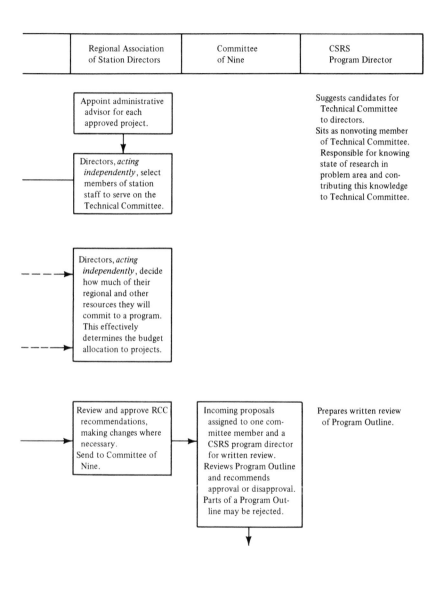

Regional Association of Station Directors	Committee of Nine	CSRS Program Director
Appoint administrative advisor for each approved project.		Suggests candidates for Technical Committee to directors. Sits as nonvoting member of Technical Committee. Responsible for knowing state of research in problem area and contributing this knowledge to Technical Committee.
Directors, *acting independently*, select members of station staff to serve on the Technical Committee.		
Directors, *acting independently*, decide how much of their regional and other resources they will commit to a program. This effectively determines the budget allocation to projects.		
Review and approve RCC recommendations, making changes where necessary. Send to Committee of Nine.	Incoming proposals assigned to one committee member and a CSRS program director for written review. Reviews Program Outline and recommends approval or disapproval. Parts of a Program Outline may be rejected.	Prepares written review of Program Outline.

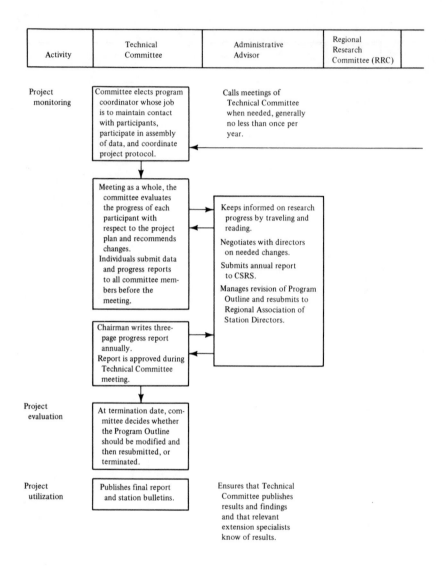

Activity	Technical Committee	Administrative Advisor	Regional Research Committee (RRC)	

Project monitoring

Technical Committee: Committee elects program coordinator whose job is to maintain contact with participants, participate in assembly of data, and coordinate project protocol.

Administrative Advisor: Calls meetings of Technical Committee when needed, generally no less than once per year.

Technical Committee: Meeting as a whole, the committee evaluates the progress of each participant with respect to the project plan and recommends changes. Individuals submit data and progress reports to all committee members before the meeting.

Administrative Advisor: Keeps informed on research progress by traveling and reading.

Negotiates with directors on needed changes.

Submits annual report to CSRS.

Manages revision of Program Outline and resubmits to Regional Association of Station Directors.

Technical Committee: Chairman writes three-page progress report annually. Report is approved during Technical Committee meeting.

Project evaluation

Technical Committee: At termination date, committee decides whether the Program Outline should be modified and then resubmitted, or terminated.

Project utilization

Technical Committee: Publishes final report and station bulletins.

Administrative Advisor: Ensures that Technical Committee publishes results and findings and that relevant extension specialists know of results.

Figure 9-1. Program Management in Regional Research Fund Programs (Continued)

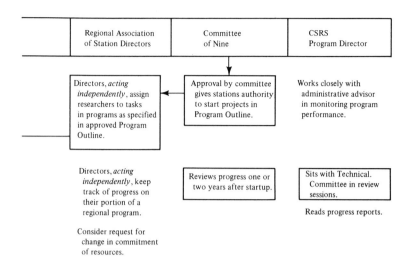

Regional Association of Station Directors	Committee of Nine	CSRS Program Director
Directors, *acting independently*, assign researchers to tasks in programs as specified in approved Program Outline.	Approval by committee gives stations authority to start projects in Program Outline.	Works closely with administrative advisor in monitoring program performance.
Directors, *acting independently*, keep track of progress on their portion of a regional program.	Reviews progress one or two years after startup.	Sits with Technical. Committee in review sessions. Reads progress reports.
Consider request for change in commitment of resources.		

Summary of Distinctive Features

The distinctive features of the Regional Research Fund method are the following:

I. Organization

Each Regional Research program is *planned and managed by a joint committee* (Technical Committee) of technical representatives from the participating stations.

II. Program Development

   A. The purpose of the Regional Research Fund method is to *coordinate efforts in several of the Experiment Stations* toward solving a common regional problem and to provide station directors with an additional *mechanism for directing the R&D priorities of Experiment Stations* toward these common problems.
   B. The program development strategy followed is to proceed sequentially through the stages of the R&D management process: (1) regional problems are analyzed to determine which are the most important; (2) a decision is made as to how available resources will be allocated to these problems; (3) a coordinated series of R&D projects is planned for each problem selected; (4) the projects are executed; and (5) the results of these projects are implemented through the Extension Service system.

III. Management Activities

   A. Program Planning
       Priorities among Regional Research programs are determined by the station directors who specify, through their Regional Associations, which problems will be addressed by regional programs; and through their stations, how much of each station's resources will be devoted to each program. Station directors base their selections among problems on information about problem severity and R&D possibilities developed by ad hoc task forces of eminent researchers appointed by the station directors.
   B. Program Management
       1. Project Generation: *The component projects within each Regional Research Fund program are planned* by the Technical Committee before the program begins, and a Program Outline is written. The *CSRS management affects the project generation process indirectly* by having a staff member serve on the Technical Committee.

2. Project Selection: *Each Program Outline is reviewed* by the Regional Research Committee, the Regional Association of Station Directors, and the Committee of Nine. The CSRS influences the review process only at the level of the Committee of Nine.

3. Project Monitoring: Each Technical Committee monitors the technical progress of its program under the guidance of an administrative advisor appointed by the Regional Association of Station Directors.

4. Project Utilization: Project results are implemented through the State Extension Service of the participating stations.

5. Project Evaluation: Application is sometimes made to revise and renew a regional program at its completion. The same process used to review new applications is used for these renewals, except that progress on the preceding program is carefully examined.

C. Program Evaluation

No formal methods of program evaluation are used, although progress reports are sometimes reviewed by the Committee of Nine.

10

Special Research Programs

Program Development

The Special Research Programs method of the USDA was developed by the CSRS to mount timely responses to urgent problems of national importance.[a] A good example of the kind of situation in which this method is used is the recent corn blight infestation, which within two years developed into a major threat to the U.S. corn crop.

The strategy of the Special Research Programs method in addressing such problems is to mobilize the latent research talent within the State Agricultural Experiment Stations and elsewhere through managerial action at the CSRS level. A sequential program development process is used: first, the station researchers (and others, as needed) determine program objectives and principal R&D priorities; second, project designs are prepared; and last, the R&D projects are conducted. The CSRS program managers retain responsibility for coordinating the program planning and management activities, including the selection of projects to be performed. Program plans include steps for implementing all the R&D results achieved. CSRS must obtain a special appropriation for each Special Research Program undertaken.

Organization

No formal organizational structure has been created for Special Research Programs. They are managed by the CSRS and carried out by the station personnel and other agricultural researchers on a task force basis. These task forces can more easily be staffed with the best available researchers than in most R&D management methods because there is more staffing slack in the CSRS system. This slack exists because the CSRS research stations are supported through formula grants, making it possible for station personnel to set aside their continuing work and serve on task forces without jeopardizing their project time commitments. This is an important feature of the CSRS R&D management method.

---

[a]The Regional Research Fund method was found to be inadequate for this task because of the amount of time required to plan and initiate programs.

Management Activities

The CSRS has not yet developed a single, preferred method for managing Special Research Programs, although certain management principles have proved important to success. When Special Research Programs were first introduced, the CSRS adopted a passive stance; it simply announced the availability of funds and the opportunity to submit proposals. As time went on, however, it became apparent that setting priorities and planning research activity at the CSRS level before funds are awarded were crucial to success. The CSRS's experience has been that the management procedures must be sufficiently flexible to consider all the potentially good ideas for solving recognized and unforeseen problems, but not so open as to have CSRS inundated with proposals, which would unnecessarily delay the problem-solving effort. As an example of how the CSRS applies these principles, the remainder of this section describes how the corn blight problem was addressed.

Program Planning

One CSRS program staff member was assigned as the corn blight program director with full-time responsibility for planning and managing CSRS's corn blight effort. This program director spent a major portion of the time, especially during the early months of the program, studying the corn blight problem. At the same time, CSRS leadership, using the corn blight program director as a consultant, worked to obtain the necessary special appropriation from Congress.

Shortly after the effort began, invitations were mailed to the state experiment stations and to other institutions to participate in a conference to be held within two months on the state of knowledge concerning the corn blight problem. Representatives appointed by the station directors and the heads of each participating institution were asked to present papers summarizing what was known about the problem in their fields of specialty. The participants were asked to consider how a practical solution could be achieved and to avoid specifying what basic research was needed to fill gaps in understanding unless it was critical to solving the corn blight problem. Following the presentation of these papers, the participants were divided into groups to discuss a possible program plan and the order of R&D priorities. Following the conference, state experiment stations were encouraged to continue studying the issue of priorities.

Four months after the planning effort began, a second conference was held specifically to focus on R&D priorities. For the first time, each state was asked what research it would like to conduct. At the same time, the Agricultural Research Service of the USDA was studying the same question of research priorities for the corn blight problem. The ARS managers asked their own laboratories the same question that the CSRS managers asked the stations: What are the most important corn blight problems and what contribution could your laboratory make?

When it became apparent that Congress would appropriate funds, the CSRS program director formally requested the stations and other institutions to send three lists: the level and nature of research activities directed toward corn blight under way in its facility, the most important research tasks from a national perspective, and the tasks that the station or institution was most capable of undertaking. The last two lists were to be organized in order of priority. These lists were then reviewed by the corn blight program director and integrated with the contributions made during the planning conferences to determine which stations and facilities could contribute most to the corn blight effort. Ability to think clearly about priorities, number of good ideas, and capability to produce quickly were the prime evaluation criteria. Based on his review, the program director then invited representatives of the Regional Association of Station Directors to Washington, D.C., for a final planning session.

All the priority and task lists submitted were presented to the assembled directors in a format that enabled them to identify common areas of concern. After some discussion, the suggested activities were categorized into five areas of research considered to be most important. The directors were then asked how they would recommend the allocation of the first $1 million, and then an additional $2 million, to the five areas if these amounts were available. The recommendations of this session were shared with the ARS, and a comparison of priority listings was made. In addition, a survey was conducted of the Experiment Station programs and the Regional Research Fund programs to see what current efforts could easily be converted to the effort.

The corn blight program director, in consultation with the CSRS supervisory staff, then selected nine sites to conduct research in the five areas identified. The sites were chosen by using similar criteria: proved ability to react capably in a short time and production of many good ideas in the priorities-setting phase of planning. Each of the nine sites was requested to submit a proposal indicating preferences regarding future work in its assigned area.

Program Management

When the funds became available, each site began its proposed work. The CSRS program director contacted the performing researchers frequently, checked on progress made with respect to objectives defined during the planning process, and made sure that the results obtained by one performer were transmitted to the others.

A plan for implementing the results of the corn blight research program was prepared during the R&D planning phase of activities and updated as the R&D was performed.

Program Evaluation

No formal mechanism for program evaluation was used for the corn blight program. Special Research Programs generally are not formally evaluated; however, informal communications channels provide valuable feedback by which to evaluate work performed.

Summary of Distinctive Features

Distinctive characteristics of the Special Research Programs method are as follows:

I. Organization

Special Research Programs are managed by a CSRS program director and carried out by ad hoc task forces of researchers from the Experiment Stations and other agricultural R&D facilities.

II. Program Development

A. The purpose of the Special Research Programs method is to find timely solutions to problems that suddenly assume national importance.
B. *The program development strategy used is to perform stages of the R&D management process sequentially.* When the CSRS staff determines that a problem is important enough to require a Special Research Program effort, a special appropriation is obtained from Congress. R&D priorities relevant to the problem are determined (program planning), followed by the design of projects, performance of those projects, and implementation.

III. Management Activities

A. Program Planning
    1. *Planning conferences* involving the program task forces are held, at which time the problem to be addressed with a Special Research Program is analyzed and R&D needs are developed.
    2. After these conferences, a meeting of station directors selected by CSRS is held to *recommend priorities among the R&D needs identified.*
B. Program Management
    1. Project Generation: *Designs for projects are generated by researchers* in the stations (and elsewhere) as part of the planning effort to

      develop R&D needs. These designs are then executed during the
      performance phase of a Special Research Program.

  2. Project Selection: The *CSRS program director and agency staff
     select the component projects* to be performed in response to the
     R&D priorities recommended by the station directors. They eval-
     uate potential research performers based on the quality of ideas
     contributed during the planning phases and on demonstrated com-
     petence to solve assigned problems quickly.

  3. Project Monitoring: The *CSRS program director monitors* project
     activities.

  4. Project Utilization: *A plan for implementing project results is pre-
     pared during the planning phase,* modified during the R&D phase,
     and then executed after the R&D results have been obtained.

  5. Project Evaluation: Completed projects are not formally evaluated.

C. Program Evaluation

Completed Special Research Programs are not formally evaluated by
CSRS management; feedback through informal channels is the basis
for evaluation.

11 Management Methods of the National Institute of Mental Health

History

The National Institute of Mental Health (NIMH) was authorized as an institute of the NIH in 1946. The NIMH was formed by transferring the Division of Mental Hygiene from the Public Service to the NIH and elevating the division's status to that of an institute. According to the National Mental Health Act of 1946, which founded the NIMH, the NIMH was to have a structure similar to that of the other institutes, i.e., with a director reporting to the director of NIH, authority to support both intramural and extramural research, and an advisory council with authority to recommend payment of grants.

The NIMH's founding act specified a broader range of missions for the NIMH than those of the other institutes, which were limited essentially to supporting research relevant to diseases. The NIMH was to be concerned not only with research on diseases but also with problems of a social nature, such as the mental health of a community as a whole. And, in addition to conducting research, the NIMH was to provide technical assistance to the states in the support of clinics and other treatment centers, to run demonstrations and train practitioners, and to aid the states directly in providing mental health care—all activities in which the other institutes were not involved. These broad missions allowed a much wider range of activities then were undertaken by any other NIH agency at the time, and are reflected in the NIMH's programs today.

Although the NIMH charter authorized this broad range of activities from its inception, only recently have more nontraditional elements emerged as significant activities in NIMH programs. Reasons for this delay can be found in the NIMH's early history.

Despite its service-oriented objectives, the new institute was made part of the NIH and consequently was placed within a highly research-oriented environment. The NIMH congressional authorization committees were a major element of this environment, and they strongly supported the premise that fundamental research was the most direct route to providing better treatment for disease. Because of this environment of fundamental research, the percentage of the NIMH budget allocated to service-oriented activities declined in the years just after its transfer from the Public Health Service to the NIH. For example, 80 percent of the Division of Mental Hygiene's budget of $6 million in 1948 was set aside for service[a] and 10 percent was directed toward research. By 1955, the NIMH's budget had increased to $14 million, with 47 percent of the total for research and 52 percent for service.

An effort to plan a more evenly balanced[b] and greatly expanded program for the NIMH was begun in the early 1950s at the urging of a member of the National Advisory Mental Health Council. The Council produced a comprehensive plan that proposed a broad and ambitious program for the NIMH in future years. Next came the passage of two acts: the Mental Health Studies Act of 1955, which delineated a thorough nationwide study of the field of mental health, and Title V of the Health Amendments Act of 1956, which called for applied research and evaluative studies with prompt translation of research findings to programs for the care, treatment, and rehabilitation of the mentally ill. Improving the operations of mental health institutions was specifically mentioned as a problem that the NIMH should address with funds from the Title V act.

The Mental Health Studies Act was the basis for the formation of a Joint Commission on Mental Illness and Health, which undertook a study of the nation's mental health needs. The commission's final report provided the background for the Mental Retardation Facilities and Community Mental Health Center Act of 1963, which marked a turning point in the balance at NIMH between services and research. This act provided grants for constructing and staffing community mental health facilities across the country, activities that the NIMH had not previously been authorized to conduct. As a result of this act, service-oriented expenditures rose dramatically in the NIMH—from $5 million in a total budget of $50 million in 1959 to $117 million in a total budget of $349 million in 1970. (Of this $349 million, $110 million was for research, and $122 million for training mental health practitioners.)

Title V of the Health Amendments Act provided the basis for a larger program of practice-oriented R&D studies in the NIMH. At first, this program was administered by the services division of NIMH and primarily consisted of demonstration projects in mental health institutions. In the mid-1960s, this program was transferred to the Division of Extramural Research and became the Applied Research branch. Simultaneously, there was a shift from the emphasis on demonstration to a stronger emphasis on research. The method used to manage this activity is called the *Applied Research method* (see Chapter 12). In 1971, part of the Title V fund was transferred back to the Services Division to establish an R&D grants program in the Mental Health Services Development branch. This program was oriented toward supporting R&D

---

[a]"Service" included service delivery and practitioner training.

[b]The term "balanced" refers to the allocation of resources among fundamental research, practice-oriented R&D, service, and practitioner training activities.

relevant to the problems encountered by service-oriented mental health institutions. The method currently used to manage this program is called the *Services R&D method* (see Chapter 15).

During the 1950s, the NIMH began another program of practice-oriented R&D activities in the Professional Services Branch of the Office of the Director. This program was more concerned with social problems than with the Title V projects that were oriented toward mental health institutions. The Professional Services Branch stimulated research projects in areas such as psychiatric rehabilitation, juvenile delinquency, juvenile drug addiction, mental retardation, alcoholism, and suicide. By the mid-1960s, this program had grown to some 30 projects, totaling $2.5 million.

Organization

The growth of the service-oriented and practice-oriented R&D programs in the NIMH triggered major changes in its organization during the mid-1960s. The large service- and practice-oriented component that had emerged did not match well with the traditions and programs of the other NIH institutes that were more research-oriented. To solve this problem, the NIMH was removed from the directorship of the NIH and in 1967 given the status of an independent bureau; in 1968 it became part of the Health Services and Mental Health Administration.

Other organizational changes within the NIMH were made during this same period, to emphasize the increasing commitment to social problems and practice-oriented R&D. Prior to these changes, the NIMH was organized in much the same way as other NIH institutes, i.e., according to functional categories. The major branches were for research, training, and service. Except for the service branch, the operation of these branches was similar to their counterparts in the NIH. They relied chiefly on unsolicited proposals for program direction and used a slightly modified form of Dual Review for proposal evaluation.

One of the major organizational changes made at the NIMH during this time was the addition of a new Division of Special Mental Health Programs. The activities in this division were directed toward solving social problems and expanding the work initiated by the Professional Services branch and some of the Title V projects. Units in the division included the Center for Alcohol Abuse, Center for Narcotics and Drug Abuse, Center for Suicide Prevention, and Center for Metropolitan Studies.

These centers were of one of two types. One type was called a *Coordinating Center,* which was responsible for building a coherent program in a designated social problem area by stimulating and coordinating proposals to be reviewed and funded by units in all the other NIMH divisions. The distinctive feature of these Coordinating Centers was that they had no funds for supporting

projects directly. The other type of center was called an *Operating Center.*
These centers also had responsibility for building a coherent program in a
designated social problem area, but unlike the Coordinating Centers, they had
funds to support projects. Operating Centers had authority to fund extramural
research and practitioner training projects, and some could conduct intramural
research. Thus, both kinds of centers had responsibilities that cut across the
traditional NIMH functional categories. The initial arrangement of centers has
changed over time; some of the Coordinating Centers became Operating Centers,
and one of the centers was dropped. The arrangement of centers in the Division of Special Mental Health Programs in 1972 is shown in Figure 11-1.

The next stage of evolution in the NIMH organizational structure, if current
trends continue, is that the centers oriented toward social problems will progress to division-level status and then to institute status within the NIMH. Institute status implies having a separate budget and an advisory council with authority to approve grants. The alcoholism program has already made this transition,
and the drug program is scheduled to become an institute soon.

As this brief history indicates, there is no dominant management method
in the NIMH, but rather many methods. This might be expected to occur in an
agency with a broad charter that has had such a rapid and diverse growth. Four
of these methods, which are intended primarily for managing practice-oriented
R&D, will be described in Chapters 12 through 15. Others (which are not discussed here) were created for managing fundamental research; for managing
what NIMH calls clinical research; and for delivering mental health services,
training, and construction facilities.

The practice-oriented R&D management methods described here are similar
to the NIH's Dual Review method, a situation not unexpected given the close
historical connection between the two agencies. Accordingly, these methods
are based on the project grant system, but have been modified to provide program directors with means for coping with the difficulties in managing practice-
oriented R&D.

The NIMH management methods are important to study because of their
close relationship to the project grant system and because many R&D agencies
use similar methods to manage practice-oriented R&D. The important question
still unresolved is whether the project grant system of management, which was
developed for managing basic research, is effective in managing practice-oriented
R&D. These NIMH methods illustrate some of the directions taken in providing
adjustments.

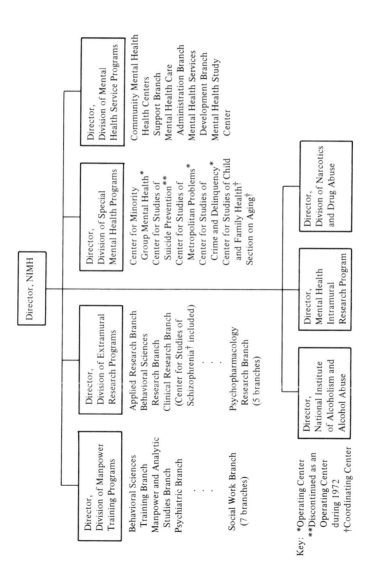

Figure 11-1. Organization of the NIMH, 1972

12 Applied Research

Program Development

The Applied Research Branch is one of five major branches in the NIMH
Extramural Research Division (see Figure 11-1). Although all branches
in the division support research, much of the practice-oriented R&D is supported by the Applied Research Branch. The remainder of the research
supported by the other branches generally is more fundamentally oriented.
The R&D supported by the Applied Research Branch is directed toward
gaining increased understanding of contemporary social problems and experi-
menting with controlled interventions as potential solutions to such problems. The purpose of the Applied Research Branch program is to support
R&D that has the potential to produce change in the provision of services
to the mentally ill, to improve social conditions, and to influence the
development of social policy. The Applied Research Branch considers
a wide range of social problems, including problems of the aged, child dis-
orders (such as hyperactivity), mental retardation, counseling, family structure, and the development of educational curricula.

Project proposals are received from university researchers in a number
of disciplines and from practitioners with diverse institutional backgrounds.
Accordingly, the list of active projects at any time covers a vast array of
social problems and practical fields. Because of this breadth, each program
director in the branch deals with a wide range of projects.

In addition to pursuing these objectives, the Applied Research Branch
also performs an important program planning function by developing
new program areas for the NIMH. These new program areas are developed
in one of several ways: The branch may stimulate project applications in
areas that the NIMH has selected as important, or it may pursue project
applications to follow up on unusually successful unsolicited projects.
Projects may also be stimulated by one of the Coordinating Centers.

It should not be assumed that the Applied Research Branch is the only
unit in NIMH responsible for developing new program areas; the origin of
some current NIMH R&D programs can be traced to activities that began
in other branches. However, new program areas can sometimes be developed more easily in the Applied Research Branch because of the wide range
of problem areas it encompasses.

93

Organization

Activity in Applied Research is divided into two program areas: juvenile problems and social problems. Each area has a review panel with an executive secretary who performs the functions of both the executive secretaries and the program directors in Dual Review. As in Dual Review, all proposals are scored by the review panel and must be approved by the National Advisory Mental Health Council. The review panels are multidisciplinary, and they include persons knowledgeable in a wide range of subject areas. In the other branches of the Extramural Research Division, the functions of the executive secretary and the program director are separated, as in Dual Review, and performed by different staff members. Unlike Dual Review, however, both staff members report to the same branch chief. Thus Applied Research is somewhat of an exception in the Extramural Division in that there is only one kind of program manager on the staff.

Management Activities

The management activities in Applied Research are also quite similar to those in Dual Review.

Program Planning

As in Dual Review, the program management staff in Applied Research has a major role in program planning. It uses essentially the same approach to planning as in Dual Review: traveling in the R&D community, attending professional meetings, and occasionally sponsoring planning workshops.

One difference between the two methods is the amount of technical assistance offered by program directors. Because the applicants for Applied Research funds include many practitioners who are not highly competent as research technicians, many of the proposals received are methodologically weak. Although some of these proposals contain unusually interesting ideas, they would ordinarily not be approved by the branch's review panels because these panels are largely made up of research specialists with high technical standards. In this situation, the program director can be selective in providing assistance to applicants to improve their proposals and thereby can have more influence over the branch's allocation priorities than ordinarily would be the case. Program directors can point out methodological deficiencies in project design, call attention to missing information, and suggest proposal formats that are appealing to the review panel. Also, when the review panel recommends disapproval but expresses interest in a revised proposal, the staff may conduct a visit to consult with the applicant–sometimes including selected members of the review panel–to assist the applicant in redesigning a proposal. The program staff in Dual Review does not have as great an opportunity to provide such technical assistance, because the applicants for fundamental research funds consist almost entirely of discipline-oriented scientists, who are, in general, highly competent in research methodology.

An important program planning difference between Dual Review and Applied Research is that program directors in Applied Research have frequent discussions with staff of other organizational units regarding program priorities. In particular, many of these discussions are with staff in the Coordinating Centers.

A third difference in planning techniques is that the program staff (branch chief, program directors, and executive secretary) meets with the review panels for part of a day every year for discussions on research trends and priorities in program development.

Project Selection. The project selection process in Applied Research is essentially the same as in Dual Review. In fact, the proposal review process begins in the NIH's Division of Research Grants (DRG), which receives all the NIMH's incoming proposals and routes them to the NIMH panels. Each panel's executive secretary assigns members of the panel as primary and secondary readers. (Typically, one primary and two secondary reviewers are assigned.) These reviewers are expected to prepare written reviews of their assigned proposals and to request from the executive secretary any additional data needed for a complete review. If the need for data is sufficiently great, the executive secretary may arrange for a site visit.

The review panel meets triannually to review about 30 to 40 proposals in a three-day session. Each proposal is discussed thoroughly for one-half to two hours and is approved or disapproved or deferred by the panel. The discussion is led by the primary and secondary reviewers. Proposals approved by a majority of panelists are then scored by secret ballot on a scale from 1 to 5 by each panelist. The final rating for a proposal is the average of the individual scores multiplied by 100.

For each proposal, the executive secretary writes a summary ("pink sheet") covering both the proposal and the panel's comments to be presented to the National Advisory Mental Health Council. The council meets to review the summaries of projects pending in all branches of the NIMH. However, because of the large number of proposals to be considered, the council can focus its attention on only a few of the total number. As in NIH council meetings, the program staff can bring certain proposals to the council's attention, or individual council members can request the review of any particular proposal. The remainder of the proposals are usually approved "en bloc." The procedures used are virtually the same as those of the NIH council meeting.

After action by the council, each executive secretary organizes the proposals rated by his or her panel in the order of descending score to determine funding priorities. Budget allocations for each panel are determined through discussions between the Applied Research branch chief and the director of the Research Division. On the average, approximately one-third of the applications considered are recommended for approval, but most of the approved applications are funded.

Project Monitoring. Monitoring of performance during the time of the grant is primarily accomplished by reading and commenting on the annual progress reports that all grantees must submit. The program staff also visits the sites of selected projects to check on progress, especially when requested to do so by the investigator. Copies of all papers and reports written by a grantee are available for the appropriate panel to use when evaluating the grantee's subsequent application for support. The quality of these outputs is considered important in the rating of any new proposals.

Process Overview. A diagram of the program management processes described in this section is presented in Figure 12-1.

Program Evaluation

No formal modes of program evaluation are used.

Staffing

The staffing pattern in the Applied Research method is essentially the same as in Dual Review. Program directors and review panelists have generally the same qualifications and duties, and the National Advisory Mental Health Council is constituted in the same way.

The only difference is in the way replacements are selected for the review panels. The executive secretary prepares a list of nominations through discussions with other members of the branch staff, the leaders of the Division of Extramural Research programs, the current review panel members, and others. These nominations are reviewed by an internal staff committee and then approved by a committee consisting of the NIMH director, the division directors, and other NIMH top management.

Summary of Distinctive Features

The distinctive features of the Applied Research method are the following:

I. Program Development

A. *Individual R&D projects are supported that are relevant to a wide range of social and mental health problems. Most of these projects begin as unsolicited proposals* from the R&D community and from the practitioner community.

B. *The program is (partly) intended as a means of supporting R&D activity in problem areas in which the NIMH wants to stimulate more research effort.*

II. Organization

A. R&D activities in Applied Research are divided into two problem areas: juvenile problems and social problems. Each problem area is managed by an executive secretary and a review panel.

B. The executive secretaries are responsible for program planning; the panel, for proposal evaluation.

III. Management Activities

A. Program Planning
   1. Program directors discuss R&D priorities with their review panels as a means of developing and implementing R&D priorities. Otherwise, *program planning activities are the same as in Dual Review.*
   2. Because the applicants are frequently practitioners who generally are not skilled in research methodology, *the program directors can have some additional influence on program priorities by differentially providing technical advice in proposal preparation.*

B. Program Management
   1. Project Generation: *Most proposals are generated by researchers or practitioners and submitted as unsolicited proposals*; some are encouraged by program management.
   2. Project Selection: Each proposal is subjected to *two formal reviews.* One review is by a technical review panel and one by the National Advisory Council.
      Project selection is dominated by the peer review panels because the priority scores they assign essentially determine the order of funding among proposals.
   3. Project Monitoring: Project performers are required to submit annual progress reports, which the program directors read and comment upon.
   4. Project Evaluation: Records of all papers and reports produced on projects are maintained for use in reviewing subsequent proposals submitted by the same investigators.

C. Program Evaluation
   No formal program evaluation procedures are used.

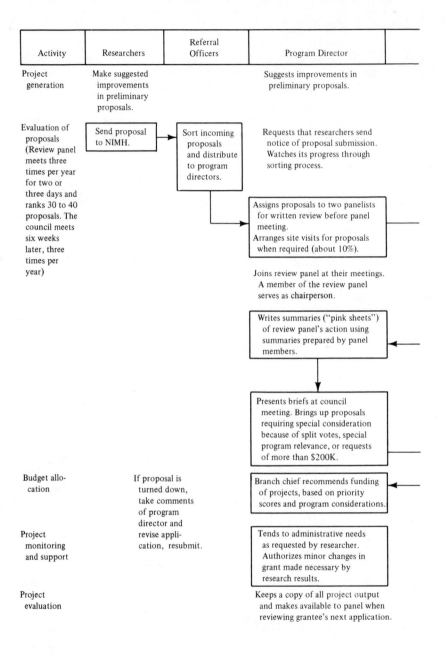

Activity	Researchers	Referral Officers	Program Director	
Project generation	Make suggested improvements in preliminary proposals.		Suggests improvements in preliminary proposals.	
Evaluation of proposals (Review panel meets three times per year for two or three days and ranks 30 to 40 proposals. The council meets six weeks later, three times per year)	Send proposal to NIMH.	Sort incoming proposals and distribute to program directors.	Requests that researchers send notice of proposal submission. Watches its progress through sorting process.	
			Assigns proposals to two panelists for written review before panel meeting. Arranges site visits for proposals when required (about 10%).	
			Joins review panel at their meetings. A member of the review panel serves as chairperson.	
			Writes summaries ("pink sheets") of review panel's action using summaries prepared by panel members.	
			Presents briefs at council meeting. Brings up proposals requiring special consideration because of split votes, special program relevance, or requests of more than $200K.	
Budget allocation	If proposal is turned down, take comments of program director and revise application, resubmit.		Branch chief recommends funding of projects, based on priority scores and program considerations.	
Project monitoring and support			Tends to administrative needs as requested by researcher. Authorizes minor changes in grant made necessary by research results.	
Project evaluation			Keeps a copy of all project output and makes available to panel when reviewing grantee's next application.	

Figure 12-1. Program Management in Applied Research

Review Panel Members (10 to 16 per panel)	Advisory Council Members (12-16)

Prepare written reviews of assigned proposals.

Meet as a group, discuss each proposal in turn. Consider site-visit report if any. Make changes in proposed budget level, if needed.

After discussing, approve or disapprove modified proposal by majority vote of the panel. Then score proposal on a 1-to-5 scale by considering scientific merit, feasibility, and competence of principal investigator. (Score of proposal is average of scores assigned by each member multiplied by 100.)

Discuss the proposals requiring attention one at a time. Ratify review panel score or modify proposal and rescore.
Members bring up any other proposal they wish to discuss.
Over 95% of proposals ratified *en bloc*.

13 Coordinating Center

Organization

A Coordinating Center is a distinctive form of organizational unit that the NIMH has devised for coordinating R&D projects relevant to a particular social or mental illness problem area. A Coordinating Center has a program staff but does not have authority to fund R&D projects;[a] its projects are funded by other organizational units in NIMH. The staff uses a variety of planning techniques compatible with the NIMH project-grant management system. In effect, the center staff is a *planning team operating at the program level* to link and develop R&D activities in a particular program area that cuts across the problem areas of other NIMH organizational units. In the organizational hierarchy, a Coordinating Center is approximately equal to an NIMH branch.

Each center is led by a director[b] with a staff of one or more program assistants. A typical staff has between one and three assistants, and the total number is rarely greater than ten. Some of the center directors have exceptional reputations as researchers in their center's problem areas, and these individuals generally believe that this is important in being able to deal successfully with program staffs and review panels in other parts of the NIMH. The Coordinating Center staff must be able to convince other organizational units of the NIMH to displace some of their own projects with Coordinating Center projects, and the center director's capabilities can be an important factor in working with these units to accept center projects.

The organization of Coordinating Centers varies considerably, although some characteristics are shared by all of them:

Coordinating Centers have authority to plan and stimulate projects in all three functional NIMH divisions: research, practitioner training, and service, although most centers emphasize activities in the research division. Centers are concerned with a mental illness or social problem area, rather than a particular scientific discipline.

None of the centers have proposal review or advisory committees.

Centers do not have budgets to support R&D projects.

---

[a]Each center has a small amount of funds for contract services.

[b]In the NIMH, the standard terminology is "center chief" instead of "program director."

Organizational differences among the centers are as follows:

> Some centers are concerned with a problem area that is relatively narrowly defined (e.g., schizophrenia); others deal with a problem area that is much broader (e.g., child and family mental health).
> Some centers are concerned with problems of mental illness and therefore do not need to coordinate as much with other federal R&D agencies.
> Some centers report organizationally to units within the Division of Extramural Research Programs and thus tend to be more research-oriented; some report organizationally to units within the Division of Special Mental Health Programs and tend to be more evenly distributed in orientation among research, training, and service.

Program Development

The Coordinating Center is designed to be an instrument for accelerating the development of a quality R&D program in an important problem area where the current R&D approaches are not well defined and where R&D has not been particularly useful in solving problems. In most cases, Coordinating Centers are not established unless the NIMH already has R&D activity under way that is in some way relevant to the problem area with which the center would be concerned.

The NIMH's reasons for establishing a Coordinating Center rather than a new branch are to reduce the chances that one R&D approach to a problem would dominate too soon in the development of an R&D program and discourage competing R&D approaches. The method encourages a diversity of R&D approaches, because the centers generally, though not always, find it easier to work with several branches rather than with a single branch in developing a program. This is because the addition of a few projects to the programs of several branches is relatively easy for the center to accomplish compared to the addition of many projects to one branch.

It should not be implied that centers are established in one particular problem area and not another solely for research reasons. An additional reason, for example, can be the existence of an interagency task force or presidential commission charged with developing recommendations for governmental action in a problem area. A Coordinating Center is a low-cost and highly visible way for the agency to manage a substantive contribution to the efforts of the task force or commission, and to demonstrate the agency's capabilities in the problem area, should a major research effort be recommended.

Management Activities

All the Coordinating Centers do not use the same management procedures, but it is not worthwhile to try distinguishing different subtypes of their management methods. The method described below is a synthesis of techniques used in several centers.

Program Planning

The approach to program planning used by the center director and staff is very similar to that used in fundamental research management methods, although the center staffs are generally more interested in developing new approaches to problems than with building a balanced program. This is because they do not have sole responsibility for the agency's effort in their problem area.

In general, the approach to planning—developing and implementing program priorities—in Coordinating Centers is qualitative and, for the most part, unstructured. As in the fundamental research management methods and the Applied Research method, no formal program plans are prepared. The Coordinating Center staff travels frequently in the R&D community to visit with potential research performers, present seminars to a variety of audiences, and attend professional meetings. Unlike the fundamental research methods, however, the center staff may also travel in the practitioner community as a means of discerning problems from the users' point of view.

Also, the center staff monitors project activities throughout the NIMH by reading the summaries of review panel evaluations (pink sheets). One purpose of this monitoring is to record the priorities of the R&D community in the center's problem area derived from the distribution of grant applications. The staff can then extend efforts in those areas where the disparities are greatest between the R&D community's and the staff's priorities. Another purpose of the monitoring activity is to look for project proposals that are in one of the center's priority areas. Depending on the situation, the center staff may want to discuss the importance of a project with the program director who is funding it in order to provoke interest in pursuing similar projects; or if the project's score is low, the center staff may explore ways to improve the project proposal.

An important planning activity of the center staff is working with the program staffs and review panels of other branches in the agency on program priorities. The center staff sometimes makes presentations on program priorities to review panels that process the center's proposals, and may bring specific problems before the panels in order to obtain their advice and gain their interest. The staff may also try to encourage the branch program staffs to help stimulate proposals in center priority areas.

The center staff may also work with the branch executive secretaries in the selection of replacement panelists. The experience has generally been that a center's proposals tend to be more favorably reviewed if two or three of a panel's members are contributors to fields that a center wants to emphasize.

Another planning activity involves coordinating the center's projects with those of other agencies concerned with the same problem areas. This can be a major activity in those centers concerned with problem areas that are emerging as important in several different agencies.

Program Management

Project Generation. The center staff is more aggressive in recruiting potential applicants and assisting in the development of projects than the program staff in the Applied Research method. At least four different techniques are used to implement program priorities:

> *Small workshops,* in which a number of researchers and potential researchers in a field are brought together to discuss methodological issues pertaining to a priority area and possible projects within it.
> *Personal visits* and presentation of seminars at universities and elsewhere to generate interest in the center's program.
> *A technical journal* published by the center. The journal contains technical articles, state-of-the-art review papers, brief summaries of negative findings, announcements, and papers suggesting directions for R&D activities. Often the center director writes an editorial highlighting particular issues and R&D projects considered most important. The editorial is written in such a way that readers will infer what further studies are needed to settle the important issues raised.
> *Direct collaboration* between the center staff and a researcher in the field. When the quality of R&D conducted in a field is especially low and the R&D community is generally pessimistic about doing work in the field due to years of fruitless effort, the center staff may enlist the aid of an extramural collaborator and jointly write a proposal. The proposal is then submitted for funding through the usual agency channels.

Project Selection. All the centers' projects are assigned by a DRG referral officer in the NIH to an NIMH branch and are evaluated in that branch by the method described in the "Project Selection" section of Applied Research (Chapter 12). Proposals from Coordinating Centers compete with all other proposals rated within an NIMH branch and are interspersed with them according to priority score when the order of funding is determined.

Project Monitoring. Most projects are monitored by the separate NIMH branches, although the center may closely monitor selected projects considered to be especially important.

Project Utilization. The journal published by the center is an important vehicle for disseminating project results. Although designed for researchers, the journal is written at a level that students and practitioners can understand. It is sent to scientists, clinicians, and lay people, and serves as a vital link among these communities and between the communities and the center.

Summary of Distinctive Features

The distinctive features of the Coordinating Center method are the following:

I. Organization

    A. The center staff consists of a director and a number of managerial assistants (from one to ten) who are responsible for planning and coordinating a program of R&D projects to be evaluated, selected, and funded by the agency branches.

    B. The center has no funds for supporting R&D projects.

II. Project Development

The center is essentially *a planning team* responsible for developing a new R&D approach in an important practical problem area where the current R&D approaches are not well defined and where R&D has not been particularly useful in solving problems.

III. Management Activities

    A. Program Planning
        1. The *center staff works with branch program staffs* in developing and implementing program priorities.
        2. A *variety of planning activities* may be undertaken, including discussions with researchers and practitioners, discussions with review panels in the branches, planning conferences, and coordination with other agencies concerned with the same problem area.

    B. Program Management
        1. Project Generation: *Considerable effort is exerted to develop proposals in specific areas* through workshops, publication of a professional journal, and direct collaboration on preparation of proposals.
        2. Project Selection: Center projects are reviewed and scored by the separate NIMH branches, using the normal panel review procedures.
        3. Project Monitoring: The center may closely monitor selected projects.

4. Project Utilization: The center uses its technical journal to disseminate project results.
5. Project Evaluation: Project renewal reviews are the only formal evaluation mechanism.

C. Program Evaluation
No formal program evaluation procedures are used.

14 Operating Center

Organization

A third management method in the NIMH is the Operating Center. Like a Coordinating Center, an Operating Center has a director and a program staff who have responsibility for developing a coherent program of R&D activities in a particular social problem area. But, unlike a Coordinating Center, an Operating Center has a technical review panel (some Operating Centers have more than one review panel) and authority to fund projects. In these respects, the organization of an Operating Center is similar to that of an Applied Research Branch. The two differ in that an Operating Center can support practitioner training projects and demonstration projects as well as R&D projects. Furthermore, some of the centers have a small intramural research staff, although these staffs generally have not been involved in extramural program management.

Unlike Coordinating Centers, all Operating Centers are in the NIMH's Division of Special Mental Health Programs. Each center director reports directly to the division director and has stature roughly equal to a branch director in the other NIMH divisions. The budget for a center is approximately the same as that of a branch.

Program Development

An Operating Center's program development responsibility is different from that of a Coordinating Center because Operating Centers have overall responsibility for an entire problem area and most of the agency funds for that area, whereas Coordinating Centers are primarily concerned with program planning. The Operating Centers, therefore, need to establish a broader range of program activities than merely program planning—they should be concerned with all stages of program development, including achieving changes in practice.

The program development strategy in Operating Centers is basically to support a number of interesting and relevant research or demonstration projects and then to follow up on these projects that are successful with the next logical step toward implementation. Most initial projects are unsolicited. This strategy calls for investing some funds on interesting but unproved ideas and the remainder on converting the ideas that are sound into workable innovations. For example, if a research or demonstration project determines that a certain way of using

107

citizen volunteers as intervention agents appears to be effective in combating a problem, there would be an evaluation project to verify the results, a development project to generate a curriculum for training the volunteers, and training projects to train the volunteers. The center might also want to investigate whether the same approach, or a modified one, would be effective for different target populations. The centers would rely on grant proposals submitted by outside investigators for all these projects; therefore, dissemination of program and project priorities is one of the most important center activities.

This program development strategy is clearly dependent on the center's authority to support different project types, ranging from research grants to training grants.

Management Activities

Program Planning

The budget of an Operating Center is typically not very large when compared to the dimensions of its problem area, so the goal of mounting coordinated programs makes it particularly necessary to define priorities and to concentrate resources on those priorities. For example, Operating Centers have been organized in the following problem areas: minority-group mental health, suicide prevention, crime and delinquency, alcoholism, and drug abuse. The possibilities for conducting R&D in these areas are great compared to the budget of most centers, which is approximately $10 million.

The center staff develops program priorities through a variety of program planning activities, including many of those used in the Applied Research and Coordinating Center methods. As in these methods, the Operating Center staff travels in the R&D and practitioner communities and attends professional meetings. In addition, the staff frequently invites a consultant to come in for a day or two to discuss program priorities.

The Operating Center staff spends a great deal of time working directly with the center review panel(s) on program priorities. The first day of each three-day review session (three sessions per year) is set aside for discussion of program objectives, the significance of past and prospective project outcomes, the overall funding situation, and other issues important to program direction. These discussions are one of the staff's principal means of influencing the center's allocation priorities, because the center usually follows the panel's recommendations regarding which projects should be supported. To the extent that the staff can influence the panel's priorities, the staff has a greater effect on program direction. The interaction works both ways, however, because the staff is also influenced in its thinking by the opinions of the panelists.

These sessions on program priorities are conducted informally with open discussion among the panel members and the staff. The center chief, who chairs the meeting with an elected member of the panel as cochairperson, attempts to keep the discussion relevant to selected topics and prevent situations in which one panel member dominates the discussion. To promote better interaction at these meetings, the program staff usually prepares an issue paper on the items for discussion, which describes the current state of affairs and outlines alternatives for the panel to consider.

As an example of the kind of issue considered at these panel meetings, one Operating Center discussed with its panel the value of verbal conditioning techniques as a means of treating deviant behavior. The panel came to the conclusion that although verbal conditioning experiments are scientifically interesting, in part because the methodology is well developed, the techniques have not proved effective in practical applications relevant to its problem area, and therefore such projects should not be supported in its center. As a result of this discussion, the panel assigned much lower scores for verbal conditioning experiments than it did previously.

Most of the Operating Centers prepare a written statement of their program objectives as a product of their planning activities. These objectives are disseminated widely in the R&D community as a means of generating interest in the priority areas. The objectives are fairly specific as to the kinds of projects that the center wants to fund and are rewritten and redistributed on a regular basis.

Program Management

The program management process in the Operating Centers is similar to that of Applied Research, except for a few differences. Stimulation of research proposals—project generation—is a more important part of program management for the Operating Centers. Specific projects are needed to move an idea from one stage of development to the next, or to investigate a particularly interesting research possibility. Stimulation of proposals is largely accomplished by personal contact, using many methods including personal visits, lectures, and distribution of publications. Project applications in priority areas are also stimulated through the review panelists and former panel members, who have strong linkages to potential R&D performers. Center chiefs work hard to expand their range of contacts with the scientific community, and they develop lists of people interested in working on particular problems to be used as the need arises.

Project proposals are evaluated using the same technique as in Applied Research. The technical panel reviews all proposals and assigns numerical scores. These results are reviewed by the NIMH Advisory Council. The center then funds approved proposals in the order of priority score until the budget is exhausted. Projects are not grouped by objectives in this process.

Grantees are somewhat more closely monitored by Operating Center staff than they are in Applied Research. After the first year of the grant, all investigators are asked to state how their research will be useful in solving one of the center's problems, and the center responds to these statements. Grantees also submit annual progress reports and may receive a call from the center chief at any time to discuss progress. One year before the termination date of a grant, the center chief gives grantees advice on items that should be included in final reports.

Summary of Distinctive Features

The distinctive features of the Operating Center method are as follows:

I. Organization

    A. The center staff consists of a program director, a number of managerial assistants, and a review panel. The panel is managed by the center staff.

    B. Some centers also have a small intramural staff, but it is not integrated with program management.

    C. Each center has authority to fund R&D grants, practitioner training grants, and demonstration grants.

II. Program Development

    A. The center is responsible for developing a *coordinated program of R&D and implementation activities* addressed to important practical problems in a defined problem area.

    B. The program development strategy is essentially to fund a variety of research and demonstration projects (primarily unsolicited) that promise important results and then to follow up on successes with projects to achieve implementation.

III. Management Activities

    A. Program Planning
        Qualitative planning techniques are used. The center staff discusses program priorities with the center's review panel, selected consultants, and other members of the R&D and practitioner communities.

    B. Program Management
        1. Project Generation: The stimulation of projects to perform specific tasks is an important aspect of program management. Techniques

similar to those used in all the other NIMH methods are used; the contacts provided by the review panel are also helpful.

2. Project Selection: Proposals are reviewed by the center's review panel using the same system as in Applied Research. All center projects are funded in order of priority score.

3. Project Monitoring: Project investigators are not closely monitored.

4. Project Utilization: The center has authority to support practitioner training projects and uses this authority as an aid in project utilization.

5. Project Evaluation: Renewal reviews are the only evaluation mechanism.

C. Program Evaluation
No formal evaluation procedures are used.

15 Services R&D

History

During the past five years, managers of the NIMH's Mental Health Services Development branch of the Division of Mental Health Service Programs have developed a distinctive method for managing R&D, which we call the Services R&D method. This method is the product of several stages of development starting from a management method similar to that of Applied Research.

The development of the Services R&D method is unique among all the R&D management methods included in this book in that each successive alteration of the method has been stimulated by the results of research and evaluation.

The first stage in the evolution of Services R&D was brought about by an evaluation project which showed that a written statement of findings was available from only 40 percent of all completed projects funded by the Mental Health Services Development branch. The corrective measure applied at this point was careful monitoring of grantee performance to assure that a final report was produced.

A subsequent evaluation project revealed that the availability of a final report from a project did not necessarily lead to the implementation of its results in many sites; less than 20 percent of the principal investigators of projects supported by the branch could name one site where their results were being used. The correction added to overcome this difficulty was a requirement that each grantee prepare a publication describing the results in terms that practitioners could understand.

About this time, research studies of the innovation process in mental health showed that less than 9 percent of the innovations adopted in mental health institutions were stimulated by written materials. In response to this finding, an effort was initiated to develop and apply a number of special techniques for supporting the utilization of R&D results. Also, grantees were told at the beginning of their projects to prepare a plan for disseminating project results and were required to carry out this plan (with any needed revisions) at the end of their projects. The special techniques for utilization developed by the branch, or any other appropriate means, could be used by the grantee. A realization gradually emerged from this approach, however, that many of the R&D results being produced by the branch solved different problems than the ones that were important to practitioners. Therefore, additional modification in R&D management methods was needed.

Program Development

The modification in management method, which is currently being refined within the branch, is to emphasize achievement of organizational change. The utilization program mentioned earlier is still retained, but the role of program staff at the NIMH is substantially altered from one of managing a grant program and stimulating adoption of results to one of finding organizations with conditions favorable to change and then arranging whatever technical assistance is needed in order to help the organization solve its problems. The program staff uses available R&D results to the extent possible in providing technical assistance, but also encourages R&D activities in problem areas where there is general concern and a lack of relevant R&D results.

Accordingly, the program development strategy used is for the program staff to be concerned, first, with needs assessment and, second, with finding ways of meeting the needs uncovered, which may include stimulating and supporting R&D. This strategy in many ways is the reverse of the strategy of the other NIMH methods, which is basically to support quality R&D and then to implement the results.

The method for implementing this program development strategy is based in the project grant method of R&D management. Project grants are awarded to individuals through their sponsoring institution to perform proposed work. The major change made in the project grant method is to shift the program staff's role from one of fostering quality R&D proposals and selecting which R&D projects to support to one of diagnosing user's problems and supporting their problem-solving efforts with R&D projects.

Organization

This organizational change strategy of program development is also reflected in the way that the Services R&D staff is internally organized. A strong emphasis is placed on maintaining a flexible and nonhierarchical organizational structure. The program staff has 15 members, each of whom is assigned a substantive or administrative area of responsibility. These areas, shown in Figure 15-1, are not rigidly defined but overlap to encourage staff interaction and exchange of resources. The staff members are clustered into five groups: four of the groups are primarily concerned with program substance and one with administration and management. Each group is led by a group coordinator, but this position is filled by members of the group on a rotating basis. The coordinator convenes the subgroup of mutual planning efforts, coordinates the group's planning activities, and handles administrative chores. The job of branch coordinator is filled jointly by the branch chief and the grants administrator.

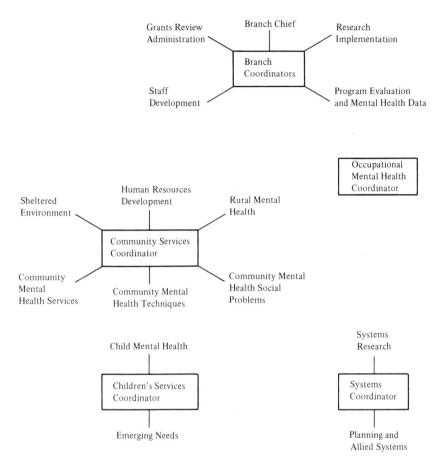

Figure 15-1. Organization of the Services R&D Branch of the NIMH

The organizational-change approach to management is also reflected in an emphasis on professional staff development activities within the branch. Bi-weekly staff meetings are held to exchange managerial, organizational, and sometimes communication problems, and to learn management skills. Courses and manuals for learning organizational change techniques have been developed as branch projects and are used by the staff in their work. A journal (*Innovations*) is produced by the branch, and staff members are asked to write articles on their respective specialties as a means of encouraging staff members to maintain their substantive expertise.

Management Activities

Program Planning

Any of the planning techniques used in the other NIMH methods can be employed in the Services R&D method, but there are some additional techniques as well.

The main techniques used by the program staff for needs assessment is traveling in the practitioner community to look for opportunities where R&D can be effective. The program staff searches for situations in which the members of a user institution are dissatisfied with its current condition, and where a political environment exists that will support change. Other factors to consider are the availability of local resources to support the change and strong leadership in the institution. The staff is also aware of what R&D results are available and looks for situations in which these results will be useful. Research on the change process supported by the branch and other agencies has shown that all these factors are important for change to occur in an institution.

Traveling in the practitioner community is feasible in the Services R&D method because there are a limited number of institutions with which the branch is primarily concerned: the NIMH's Community Mental Health Centers and other mental health institutions. If the number of institutions were much larger, for example, as the number of school districts in the country, traveling in the practitioner community to determine needs would probably not be as effective.

When attending professional meetings of R&D performers or practitioners, the program staff often circulates a small survey form to obtain views regarding critical R&D areas. The branch has found this to be a useful device for measuring the extent of concern for mental health problems. The branch has also found that researchers often have very different perceptions of problems from those of practitioners.

Another method of needs assessment that the branch uses is to contract for evaluations of community mental health services, particularly to assess impacts and access. The staff also encourages institutions to conduct their own evaluations.

Another method of needs assessment is now in the design stage: a system for collecting biometric data on populations in mental health facilities across the country. The staff will analyze the data from this system as a means of problem diagnosis.

The results of all these activities are discussed by the program staff and formulated into R&D priorities. The staff then solicits R&D proposals in the priority areas using techniques shared by the other NIMH methods: publications, personal contacts, and branch review panels.

The program staff is able to perform many of these activities because the project work load per staff member is lighter in the Services R&D method than in the other NIMH methods. Typically, each program director has four new grants per year, and no more than seven active grants at any time.

Each program staff member is responsible for coordinating project activity within her or his program area in a number of ways. One responsibility is to have the active projects in the area reflect the branch priorities and be derived from specific needs of practitioners. In addition, there should be sufficient dissemination and utilization mechanisms built into each project, and the director should be responsible for stimulating auziliary mechanisms if necessary. The director is also responsible for developing collaborative projects on different aspects of a problem whenever it appears desirable.

Project Generation. All grant applications are prepared by the proposing investigator, but the program staff stimulates some of the proposals received. Any of the techniques used in the other NIMH methods or in the fundamental research methods may be used for this purpose.

Before investing effort in stimulating a proposal, however, a program staff member searches the literature and uses professional contacts to see if a solution has already been proposed and tested. The staff member may also use the NIMH's computer information system to search through completed NIMH projects. Other literature screening services may also be used, but in Services R&D, solutions are not always in the open literature because many projects are performed by practitioners or administrators who have neither the time nor the incentive to publish their results in the journals. Articles are solicited from these people, however, to be included in the branch publication, *Innovations.*

Project Selection. Project selection is performed in almost the same manner as it is in the Operating Centers. The primary review panel meets four times per year for two or three days each time. One of the sessions and part of each of the remaining sessions are allotted to discussion of program priorities.

Project Monitoring. Once a project is funded, the grantee's performance is monitored by a program staff member who visits the grantee every eight or nine months to discuss progress. At each of these meetings, the staff member asks the grantee what she or he expects the final results will be and how they will be disseminated. The program staff member offers guidance in preparing a dissemination plan and the final report. The branch has adopted this policy because its research has shown that investigators who plan for dissemination of results from the beginning of their project are much more likely to have their results used in practice. For this same reason, the branch includes a questionnaire with each application form mailed to a potential grantee. It contains questions such as: What information did the project yield that would be of value to others? By what method were results obtained? What dissemination efforts were completed? Who is using the results? The same questionnaire is sent to the grantee after six months of a project have elapsed as a reminder that he or she will be held accountable for dissemination at the end of the project, when again the grantee is asked to fill out the questionnaire. By this technique, the percentage of projects yielding final reports has increased from 40 to 95 percent, and the number of projects reporting adoption of results by others has risen from 19 to 50 percent (based on internal staff studies of the Services R&D branch). As discussed previously, each project investigator is expected to design and implement a utilization plan for the project, and program directors counsel investigators on preparing these plans.

Project Utilization. The program directors are in a position to advise grantees on the best ways to disseminate project results, since over the years research on this subject has been conducted by the NIMH's Mental Health Services Development branch, and a set of tested methods of utilization mechanisms is available for use in specific situations. The branch leadership can also facilitate adoption directly because it has the budget to fund demonstrations, training activities, and other aids to utilization.

Program Evaluation

Rather than evaluating its program directly, the Services Development branch evaluates each program staff member's performance using a "goal attainment scale." At the beginning of each year, the program director, in consultation with the branch chief and staff, decides on a number (usually about five) of specific work objectives for the coming year. For each objective, five levels of achievement are reported in terms of specific outcomes. The levels of attainment are assigned integer values from –2 to +2. Each objective is then assigned a weight from 0 to 10. At any time, a program director's "attainment score" is simply the product of each objective's weight factor multiplied by its level of attainment, summed over all objectives.

The program directors and branch leadership revise these rating schedules quarterly, but progress is evaluated by the branch chief annually. Progress toward each program director's objectives is one of the items discussed at the biweekly staff meetings. By discussing progress in joint sessions, directors obtain more objective perceptions of progress in their own program areas.

Summary of Distinctive Features

The distinctive features of the Services R&D method are the following:

I. Program Development

An organizational-change approach to program development is used: the strategy is, first, to determine perceived needs and the potential for change in practitioner organizations and, second, to search for workable solutions to satisfy those needs, stimulate necessary R&D, and encourage dissemination and utilization of results.

II. Organization

A. The branch using the Services R&D method is divided into five working groups: a leadership group and four problem area groups. Each group consists of from one to five program managers. The branch chief is the head of the leadership group, but the responsibility of heading the problem-area groups is shared by the members of a group on a rotating basis.

B. The branch has authority to fund R&D projects and demonstrations.

III. Management Activities

A. Program Planning
Qualitative planning techniques are used primarily, except that the emphasis is on determining needs in the user community as the basis for setting program priorities.

B. Program Management
1. Project Generation: The program staff makes a thorough search of completed work before stimulating an R&D project.
2. Project Selection: R&D projects are, in effect, selected by a peer-review panel, although the program staff works with the panel to obtain prior agreement on program priorities.
3. Project Monitoring: All projects are monitored by means of a site visit at least once per year. Grantees are sent a notice to remind them to plan and execute a utilization effort at the end of their projects.
4. Project Utilization: Grantees are expected to implement their project results at several sites.
5. Project Evaluation: Renewal reviews are the only evaluation mechanism used.

C. Program Evaluation
Each program director establishes performance objectives and is evaluated with respect to these objectives annually.

16 Research and Evaluation

History

Although the Office of Economic Opportunity (OEO) is currently being phased out as an agency, primarily by transferring its programs to other federal departments, one of their R&D management methods, developed and used in the past few years, remains a viable alternative for all agencies conducting R&D. Accordingly, this chapter describes, in the past tense, the OEO management method that was used just before the time of transfer.

Like the Department of Agriculture and the National Institute of Mental Health, OEO supported both R&D and action programs in carrying out its mission, and like these agencies, action programs constituted a larger portion of its activities than R&D. In fiscal year 1971, for example, OEO spent $100 million on R&D and $794 million on action programs.

The OEO budget for R&D has increased as a proportion of the total budget over the last several years. A major shift in this direction occurred in 1969 when OEO was reorganized and it was announced that OEO's prime responsibility in the future would be to develop and test new programs, which would then be transferred to other agencies for implementation and operation. In addition, OEO was to assume a larger role in analyzing domestic policy issues for the Executive Office of the President. Thus, OEO was to have a dual role in providing staff to the Executive Office of the President on policy issues and producing verified, new programs.

Organization

The management method discussed in this chapter describes how OEO's R&D division, the Office of Planning, Research, and Evaluation (PR&E), performed the dual role mentioned. PR&E has pioneered in the use of carefully planned and evaluated social experiments as a means of developing new social programs and policy-relevant information. R&D was conducted in other OEO divisions, but generally not with the highly disciplined approach used in PR&E. These other OEO divisions were primarily involved in arranging pilot programs and demonstrations.

The other major divisions of OEO and their funding levels were the Office of Operations ($360 million in fiscal year 1971), Office of Legal Services ($62 million), Office of Health Affairs ($100 million), and the Office of Program Development ($52 million). The *Office of Operations* supervised OEO's Regional Offices and the Community Action Agencies funded by Title II of the OEO Act. It engaged in a small amount of decision-oriented research directed toward service-delivery problems. The *Office of Legal Services* had some research funds ($5 million in fiscal year 1971), which were used for decision-oriented research, preparation of briefs for operating offices, and a university center. The *Office of Health Affairs* was primarily involved in demonstrations. The *Office of Program Development* (OPD) was closest to PR&E in function. Its primary method of operation was to conduct "pattern" demonstrations and follow up with rigorous evaluations; these demonstrations were planned so that several together would contain a pattern of variations that constituted an experiment. However, OPD tended to be more action-oriented and less research-oriented than PR&E in carrying out its developmental activity.

PR&E organized its internal staff in a unique way. Three internal groups were formed, assigned by R&D function: Experimental Research, Policy Research, and Evaluation. PR&E deliberately defined these functions to be complementary in providing the full range of skills needed to manage the program development process and, at the same time, to overlap in such a way that the groups competed with each other on the details of experiment design and evaluation. Each of these groups had a staff of about 20 people. In fiscal year 1971 their respective budgets were $17 million, $6 million, and $6 million.

Programs were not designated in the formal organization chart but did exist as substantive entities, albeit entities with poorly defined boundaries in the totality of R&D supported. There were no formally designated program leaders or program units, but it was possible to identify distinct "loci" of inter-related projects and the associated staff. At any time there were several of these loci, each representing a program in a different stage of development.

The functions of the *Experimental Research group* were primarily to translate program models into actual social experiments installed and operated at real-world sites, and to monitor and support the execution of these experiments. The Experimental Research group was responsible for the following:

> *The detailed design of experiments*, including the sample design, measurement of the major dependent and independent variables in the model; selection of the experimental sites; identification of major population subgroups at the experimental sites; identification of legal, practical, and other constraints at the experimental sites; and sometimes selection of evaluation tests.
>
> *Liaison with institutions and persons at the experimental site* who would be affected by the experiment.
>
> *On-site management of the experimental projects*, or at least oversight of on-site management provided by a contractor.

Evaluation of experiment results, when the task could be accomplished with simple, well-accepted quantitative tests, such as those used for cognitive achievement.

Most of the Experimental Research staff members had graduate degrees in social science, and a few had extensive experience as practitioners; for example, they had served on a legislative staff. In general, the Experimental Research staff was experienced in the practicalities of designing and running social experiments.

The second PR&E component, the *Policy Research group*, had two functions:

Generation of basically new program ideas.
Production of policy analyses on short notice that addressed issues posed by decisionmakers in the Executive Office of the President.

The Policy Research staff was the most academic of the three PR&E groups. It was largely made up of economists, but some were sociologists, psychologists, political scientists, and computer scientists. The staff conducted research into the underlying causes of problems, with each staff member choosing a limited area of specialization (early childhood education, for example). The research undertaken was policy-oriented in that it was relevant to generating new ideas for PR&E programs and producing policy analyses. Studies of physiological development in young children, for example, would probably not have been done, but analysis of the effects of nutrition on educational outcomes perhaps would have been relevant.

The third component, the *Evaluation group*, had the following functions:

Evaluation of experiments managed by the Experimental Research Group.
Evaluation of the impact of major federal programs (such as manpower programs).
Evaluation of natural experiments.
Analysis of data collected on PR&E experiments or other federal programs.

The Evaluation group staff was made up of social scientists, statisticians, systems analysts, and operations researchers. It also included specialists in evaluation methodology and could be distinguished in its professional attitude from the two other groups by the attention given to designing experiments and evaluations that were as rigorous and complete as possible. The Evaluation group was less concerned with generating social action than the Experimental Research group, less concerned with understanding basic causes for problems than the Policy Research group, but more concerned with *measuring* how well a program or experiment was performing and how it could be improved.

The organization of the OEO is shown in Figure 16-1.

Program Development

The program development process of the Research and Evaluation method was more highly structured and sequential than are most of the other management methods discussed thus far. The most visible and unique part of the program development process was its use of large-scale experimentation in real-world environments to validate and refine program ideas. The experiments were visible because typically they were large, involving the expenditure of several million dollars, and because they were carried out in a community setting. This approach was unique in that few other practice-oriented R&D agencies employed large-scale experimentation to as great an extent in program development as did PR&E.

By viewing the program development process from a broad perspective, it can be conceptualized as consisting of the following steps:[a]

1. Identification of the problem.
2. Proposal of alternative solutions and analysis of proposed solutions using available theoretical and empirical evidence.
3. Generation and preliminary analysis of model programs.[b]
4. Detailed design of experiments and evaluations to test portions of the model programs about which there is uncertainty.
5. Execution of experiments and evaluation of these experiments.
6. Redesign of model programs.
7. Implementation of programs.

To serve as an example, these steps could have been correlated with an idealized version of one PR&E effort to improve the education received by the poor. The perception gradually emerged through research and analysis that instead of making a direct assault on the problem by finding ways to improve the instructional process, a better approach was to find ways of financing education that would have the auxiliary effect of inducing institutional changes in the schools that would make them more receptive to innovation and responsive to community needs. The supposition was that these changes would eventually result in more improvement in educational outcomes per dollar than could be obtained by more direct approaches.

With this result, PR&E had accomplished the first step in the program

---

[a]This conceptualization is drawn from conversations with Stephen M. Barro of The Rand Corporation.

[b]In many cases, this step is abbreviated, and program development proceeds to the design of experiments and evaluations. However, analysts should have an operational program in mind when selecting the factors to test with social experimentation, because the purpose of most social experimentation is to develop operational programs.

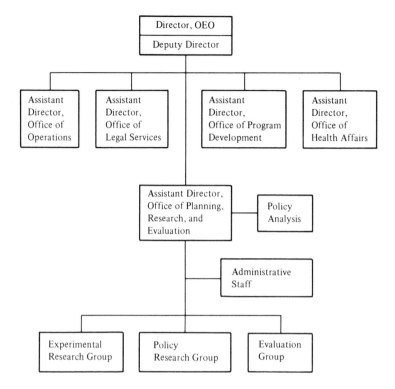

Figure 16-1. Organization of OEO, 1972

development process, i.e., identifying the problem. As the second step, PR&E identified and analyzed several alternative solutions to this problem based on the idea of financing education through vouchers given to parents.[c] Analyzing these solutions involved postulating the different forms of vouchers and then projecting the changes that each form might produce in the institutional structure of education. Examples of such structural changes would be alterations of the incentive structures within the schools, the appearance of new suppliers of education, shifts in the distribution of students among schools, and so forth. The results of this analysis provided the basis for the third step, specifying alternative model programs for implementing the various forms of vouchers.

A model program, as defined here, is a plan for implementing an alternative solution as a real-world operational program. The level of detail in a model program would include delineation of the target group; specification of the services to be provided; and organization of service delivery, administration,

---

[c]The concept of a "basic idea" was introduced in the "Program Development" section of the Introduction to this book.

and incentive structures for both the providers and the consumers. This third step also includes several kinds of comparative analyses of these models: economic analyses to assess costs and financial impacts, organizational and sociological analyses to assess impacts on social structures, evaluations of service effectiveness, legal and political analyses to assess the feasibility of implementation. One important purpose of these analyses is to identify the major areas of uncertainty in each model and the areas that can be addressed experimentally.

In the fourth step, experiment design, portions of the various models that are uncertain in the early stages are translated into actual projects for *in vitro* experimentation. Some of the specific tasks involved in designing an experiment were described in the "Organization" section of this chapter.

The interaction between the third and fourth steps can be great, since the realities encountered in designing the experimental projects often provide additional conceptual insights that can be used to improve the model programs. The realities can also impose constraints that preclude using certain features of some of the models, thereby creating a need for redesign.

The remaining steps in the OEO program development process require less explanation. Executing the experiment, part of step 5, involved sustaining the experimental intervention over a period of time. Evaluating the experiment, the other part of step 5, involved collecting the experimental data and analyzing the results.

The sixth step was the redesign of the program models using the experimental results. The redesign step may result in an iteration leading to another round of experimentation or implementation, if any of the models have proved effective. The redesign and implementation steps will not be considered in much detail in the discussion of management activities that follows because PR&E did not exist long enough to bring many programs to this stage of development.

Management Activities

Program Planning

In strong contrast to the fundamental research methods and the other practice-oriented R&D methods, program planning in PR&E was primarily an intramural activity. The external R&D community was involved only in certain steps of the planning process or in indirect ways.

The PR&E planning process, like that of most of the previously described R&D management methods,[d] did not use a formalized set of procedures or a

---

[d]The exception is the CSRS's Regional Research Fund method.

rigid system of defining responsibilities, and detailed program plans were not prepared.

The organization of planning activities among the three internal groups within PR&E[e] is shown in Table 16-1. The first column of the table indicates the steps in the OEO program development process that we consider to be program planning activities; these are the first three steps (problem identification, generation of alternative solutions, model generation and analysis) and the sixth (redesign of models). The other columns of the table indicate the kinds of activities that each internal group performs in order to carry out each of these steps.

The staff of the Policy Research group contributed to the planning process primarily by conducting in-depth, policy-oriented research in the problem areas addressed. In conducting their research, the Policy Research staff members were expected to develop a thorough understanding of their field and to probe for fundamental relationships that helped in identifying basic problems. The director of PR&E (who was also the assistant director of the OEO) worked closely with the staff in conducting this research (1) to set the tone of the research activity, and (2) to lend insights gained from discussions in policy-making circles about what the problems were. The Policy Research group staff also contributed to the planning process by assisting in the analysis of tentative model programs and of interim results from experiments being conducted. The group also contributed to the planning process through its policy analyses for decisionmakers in the Executive Office of the President. In conducting these analyses, Policy Research staff members often gained a new perspective on the problems that they were analyzing in their planning work.

The Policy Research group provided another vital function in the Research and Evaluation method: it linked the planning process to the R&D performer community. This linkage was established by providing Policy Research group staff members with funds to award extramural research grants in areas related to their interests. Grantees provided research results relevant to the program planning process, provided a network of contacts in the research community, and were used as consultants in the program planning process. These grantees were also a means by which the Policy Research staff could keep up to date with research progress relevant to the problems being addressed. This was especially important because there were few other linkages to the R&D community in the other stages of the OEO method. In all the management methods discussed thus far, there has been a strong linkage to the R&D community at least at the project generation and selection stages of the management process.

The Evaluation group contributed to the planning process primarily by

_____

[e] As described above, the Experimental Research group, Policy Research group, and Evaluation group.

Table 16-1
Organization of Program Planning Activities in OEO

Steps in OEO Program Development Process	Activities of Organizational Units		
	Experiment Research	Policy Research	Evaluation
(1) Problem identification		Perform in-depth, policy-oriented research into underlying causes of problems.	Interpret evaluations of natural experiments and major federal programs. Analyze data collected in OEO and other programs.
(2) Generation of basic program ideas (alternative solutions). Analysis of these alternative solutions.[a]	Develop basic program ideas from experience in designing and managing experiments.	Prepare policy analyses for federal decisionmakers. Develop basic program ideas by drawing on the results of research studies into problems. Award research grants to selected performers.[b] Discuss research and problems with performers.[b]	
(3) Generation and analysis of model programs.	Work with policy research or evaluation personnel to generate and analyze models. Alternatively, contract for generation and analysis of model programs.	Generate and analyze alternative model programs. Alternatively, contract for generation and analysis of model programs.[b]	
(6) Redesign of model programs.		Perform continuing analyses of models that have been postulated. Analyze interim experimental results.	Analyze interim experimental results.

[a] Steps 1 and 2 are indistinguishable in the activities of the Policy Research and the Evaluation groups.
[b] Point of interaction between OEO staff and R&D performer community.

conducting evaluations of PR&E experiments, natural experiments, and other federal programs, and by analyzing data available from a variety of sources. The evaluation results sometimes added directly to the planning process by indicating what the distribution of effort should be among problem areas. Or, in the course of designing, conducting, and interpreting evaluation projects, staff members sometimes gained basic ideas for new programs. PR&E management guarded against losing this influence in the planning process by ensuring that there were enough members on the evaluation staff so that, on the average, 25 percent of the total effort could be spent on these activities. The danger was that pressures to design and monitor evaluations would consume all the staff's time unless management controlled the work load and staffing level.

The Experimental Research group also contributed to the program planning process since the staff on occasion generated new program ideas during the course of designing and managing PR&E experiments. A staff member who contributed one of these ideas would then work with Policy Research or Evaluation staff members to perform the other steps in the planning process. Sometimes these ideas were transferred to the Policy Research group for development into models and experiments, or a contractor was hired to develop and analyze program models. The option of hiring a contractor for this phase of program planning also applied to ideas generated in the Policy Research group.

Program Management

In addition to these organizational inputs to planning, there were managerial techniques used as well.

For example, management brought members of the three staff groups together on occasion to criticize each other's work and to make suggestions. The director of PR&E did this especially when alternative program models were being developed. The complementary skills and interests of the staffs created a kind of interaction that helped to keep all parties open to new alternatives, and helped each to recognize oversights. The result was better quality program ideas and better model formulations.

Another managerial method used was to give special emphasis to maintaining staff quality. This is exceedingly important in the Research and Evaluation method because program planning, as well as other stages of the management process, depends on the quality of the internal staff. Quality was maintained by giving constant attention to recruiting and hiring highly competent personnel, by establishing a challenging work environment, and by careful scheduling of the staff's work load. Regarding this last technique, PR&E was always careful to regulate the number of requests for policy analyses from the Policy Research group staff so that only a small portion of their time was spent on this activity. Otherwise, the Policy Research group staff could have spent too much time on

short-term policy analysis and lost its research perspective. As a means of
protecting the Policy Research group staff, the director created a buffer group,
called a Policy Analysis staff, to handle overflow requests that would be overly
burdensome. The Policy Analysis staff was a small group of generalists who
reported to the director and who were capable of doing credible analyses on
short notice. This staff is shown in Figure 16-1.

Project Generation. The fourth step in the PR&E program development
process (experiment design and evaluation design) was equivalent to project
generation. Project generation was typically a lengthy and expensive activity
in the Research and Evaluation method because the task was to translate a
conceptual model into experimental projects. Each project could involve a
large number of service providers and analysts, a sizable data collection and
processing effort, a complicated administrative structure, and so forth. As
a result, PR&E generally divided project generation into two parts:

A *preliminary phase*, in which OEO carried the project design far enough
to write an RFP (Request For Proposal) or a grant proposal.
A *design phase*, in which a contractor or grantee finalized the project
design.

The exact boundary between these phases varied with the project. In some
cases, OEO did more of the design than in others.
   Each model generated in the program planning process required at least
one project, but usually there were two, and sometimes more. Only one project
was required when the experiment and its evaluation could be combined and
when the experiment could be run at one site. As a rule, the experiment and
the evaluation were combined only when the evaluation was very simple, for
example, measuring cognitive achievement using a standardized test. When
the evaluation was more complex, both an experimental project and an evaluation project were separately funded. If the experiment were to be run at
multiple sites, a number of experimental projects were often needed.
   Both grants and contracts were used for supporting projects. Evaluations
were always supported by contract, but experiments were usually supported
by grants. Grants were advantageous when the performer was to be a public
agency (e.g., a school district or a hospital) in a situation that would make
competitive selection of a contractor impractical. Grants and contracts were
handled in almost the same manner, however, because even for grants, OEO
staff imposed a project outline that was equivalent in substantive content to
an RFP, and monitored grantees very closely. The main difference was that
grants were an easier instrument to use administratively when awards needed
to be made noncompetitively.
   PR&E's procedures for generating both experimental projects and evaluation projects were similar. The preliminary phase of project generation was

carried out by a team of at least two full-time persons; on experimental projects, there were typically between three and six full-time persons. The experimental and the evaluation project teams worked independently and were not organized under a single program leader. However, the PR&E director expected that the two groups would work on design issues together and periodically brought them together to resolve difficult issues. Interaction between the groups was enhanced by having a representative of the evaluation group participate in all visits made by the experimental project group to potential experimental sites.

The preliminary phase generally lasted for several months and culminated in RFPs (for contracts) or project outlines (for grant proposals). The project teams put considerable effort into writing the RFPs and project outlines—sometimes as many as five or more drafts were written before a final product was obtained. Successive drafts were critiqued by staff from the opposite group, the PR&E director, and the directors of the Evaluation group and the Experimental Research group. The final product specified the evaluation (experiment) design in outline form, the criteria to be used in evaluating proposals, and the weights in numerical score that each criteria would have in selecting the winning contractor(s) or grantee(s).

Project Selection. Project selection occurred at the juncture between the preliminary phase and the design phase. Even though the purpose of the design phase was to complete the project designs prior to executing the projects (the fourth step in the program development process), projects were selected at this point because in almost every project the policy was to have the contractor (grantee) that designed a project also execute it. Thus, choosing a performer for the design phase was tantamount to deciding whether PR&E's resources would be spent on a particular project and who would perform it.

The project selection process in the OEO model was essentially internal, since few non-OEO staff members were involved in the project selection decision. PR&E's process for reviewing RFPs and project outlines (for grants) began with a management-oriented review. This review was conducted by the *Project Review Board*, a standing committee that consisted of the director of PR&E's administrative staff, ten PR&E staff members (selected by the director), one representative from the General Counsel's Office, and one from OEO's office of Grant and Contract Review. The purpose of this review was to check (1) that the necessary funds had been budgeted, (2) that the project was designed to meet the objectives set for it, and (3) that the estimated cost was appropriate for the proposed project. The board also determined if a contract was the appropriate instrument and what the terms of contract should be (cost plus fixed fee, fixed price, or some other terms). The purpose of this review was to advise the PR&E director on the progress and direction of the preliminary design effort.

If the estimated project cost was over $300,000 (this was a limit that had been established by the Office of Grant and Contract Review), an *ad hoc*

Procurement Evaluation Board was convened near the end of the preliminary phase to review the final drafts of the RFP (or project outline). The board reviewed the criteria to be used in selecting the winning contractor(s) and developed an instrument for evaluating proposals with respect to the criteria. The instrument was usually a detailed list of questions that proposal evaluators could use in assigning scores for each criterion. The purpose of the board's review was to increase the assurance that the winning contractor(s) would be selected impartially. The board members were selected by the deputy director of OEO; on the board were included the director of the Office of Grant and Contract Review, the project team leader, and an agency wide cross section of seven to ten senior-level staff members.

If the estimated project cost was to be less than $300,000, the process for reviewing the criteria to be used in evaluating bidders was less formal. Rather than convening a Procurement Evaluation Board to accomplish this review, it was done by PR&E top management when they reviewed the final draft of the RFP (or project outline) for substance.

All final drafts were reviewed for their technical substance and legal conformity by OEO managers: specifically, the director of PR&E, the OEO General Counsel, and the director of the Office of Grant and Contract Review. If the RFP was acceptable to all these reviewers, the director of PR&E released it to *Commerce Business Daily*. It was also sent directly to individuals or firms that the PR&E management or staff considered potential performers. Grant proposals were prepared from project outlines by interested applicants and by the staff of potential sites identified by the experimental project team.

Grant proposals and proposals received in response to an RFP were evaluated by means of a committee review system. If the estimated project cost was over $300,000, the Procurement Evaluation Board, the same panel that had reviewed the RFP (project outline), performed the first review; if the estimated cost was less than $300,000, a new Procurement Evaluation Board was convened. The panel members were chosen by the project team leader with the approval of the Office of Grant and Contract Review. Included were the contracting officer for the project, senior-level staff people from throughout the agency, and occasionally a few experts from outside OEO.

If a contract award were to be made, the Procurement Evaluation Board members scored the proposals on technical merit according to the criteria established in the RFP. There were no standardized procedures for assigning scores, but as a general rule each RFP was read and scored by four board members. The proposal's technical merit score was the average of its reader's scores. For projects over $300,000, the board members were guided in assigning scores by the list of questions developed during the RFP writing stage; for projects under $300,000, the board operated less formally by allowing individual board members greater discretion in assigning scores. Grant proposals went through essentially the same review for technical merit, although a formal scoring procedure generally was not used.

After scores had been assigned, the board considered the cost of proposals for the first time. It then determined which set of projects were in the "competitive range," i.e., those proposals that were high in technical merit but not too expensive. On the average, about five bidders were included, but sometimes there were ten or more, especially on large procurements. The technical rating of particular proposals would sometimes be reassessed during this time.

Often the bidders in the competitive range were invited to OEO to discuss the strengths and weaknesses of their proposals with the project team, the director of the Evaluation (or Experimental Research) group, and the Office of Grant and Contract Review. During these meetings, the project team and the director of the Evaluation (or Experimental Research) group discussed technical issues and assessed the capability and commitment of each bidder. The Office of Grant and Contract Review gave bidders until a predetermined date to revise their cost, their technical proposals, or both.

Revised cost and technical proposals received from these bidders were then rescored and reevaluated by the Procurement Evaluation Board for a final determination of order according to technical merit. For this evaluation, each proposal was read and scored by each board member.

If the estimated project cost was under $300,000, the final decision on which contractor(s) and grantee(s) would be supported was made by the director of PR&E, who relied to a great extent on the judgments of the project team leaders and the contracting officers of the projects.

If the estimated project cost was over $300,000, the final decision on support was made by the *Source Selection Board*. This board consisted of the deputy director of OEO, the director of PR&E, and the General Counsel. The board heard a presentation by the project team leaders summarizing the results of the Procurement Evaluation Board deliberations. This presentation included both the Procurement Evaluation Board's findings regarding bidders that were in the competitive range and their findings on revised proposals from those bidders. After discussion, the Source Selection Board reached a consensus on the winning contractor(s) and grantee(s).

Project Monitoring. Evaluation contracts and experimental grants were very closely monitored during their performance. A $1 million evaluation would be managed full-time by a two- or three-man team, especially during the design phase. Often this was the same team that wrote the RFP. The project team was very active and aggressive in managing evaluation contractors so that the final product would satisfy OEO's needs. PR&E believed that close monitoring was essential. Experiments were monitored in the same way, with typically three to six staff members assigned full-time to each project.

If a major change in contract rules or scope was desirable during the course of an evaluation project, this need was considered by the Project Review Board and then negotiated with the contractor.

Project Utilization. At the end of an evaluation project, the contractor wrote a final report that was publicly released by PR&E. The contractor also submitted all the nonconfidential data collected on the project. PR&E's policy was to make all of this available for researchers. The project teams also wrote a report on completed projects summarizing the policy-relevant findings and indicating where additional study was needed.

Sometimes a grant or contract was awarded for this additional study. Either the project contractor, if he or she performed well, or another contractor might be selected for this work. Otherwise, the study was conducted by the PR&E staff. The need for such follow-up studies was not indicative of a poorly designed project or poor performance. Sometimes policy questions arose during the course of performance that could not be foreseen at the beginning.

PR&E's evaluation results were strongly linked with policymaking because of the relationship between the staff and the Executive Office of the President. Since the director of PR&E served on task forces and consulted with White House and OMB staff on a regular basis, she or he transmitted evaluation results directly to decisionmakers. This was an important feature of the OEO Research and Evaluation method.

Project Evaluation. Within 60 days after the close of an evaluation contract, the project team evaluated the contractor's performance and submitted a report to OEO's Office of Grant and Contract Review. These reports were filed and recalled later for use by review panels when the contractor applied again.

Process Overview. A diagram of the program management process appears in Figure 16-2.

Program Evaluation

No formal mechanisms for program evaluation were employed.

Staffing

Project Review Board

The director of PR&E chose approximately ten (the number varies over time) PR&E staff members to serve on the board which he or she chaired. In addition, representatives from the Office of Grant and Contract Review and the General Counsel's office were also present.

Procurement Evaluation Board

The deputy director of OEO chose between seven and ten senior-level staff to serve on this board. One of these members was the evaluation project team leader. Someone from the General Counsel's office, and the Procurement Office also served. A new board was chosen for each procurement reviewed.

Source Selection Board

The Source Selection Board consisted of the deputy director of OEO, the director of PR&E, and the General Counsel of OEO.

Summary of Distinctive Features

The distinctive features of the OEO method were the following:

I. Program Development

    A. *Large-scale social experimentation* played a central role in the program development process, serving as a means of developing and testing ideas for major social interventions.

    B. Experimentation was predicated on the completion of several prior steps: problem formulation, generation of alternative solutions, model program design, and experiment design.

    C. The program development process was controlled by the internal staff with minimal interaction with the external R&D community.

II. Organization

    A. Internally, the staff was *organized into three functionally oriented groups:* Experimental Research, Policy Research, and Evaluation, rather than problem- or discipline-oriented groups.

    B. Each group contributed to the development of a program in such a way that the groups mutually checked each other's performance.

III. Management Activities

    A. Program Planning

        1. *Program plans emerged from three complementary staff activities:* policy-oriented research into underlying causes of problems, evaluations of attempted social interventions, and invention based on experiences gained in attempting to manage social interventions.

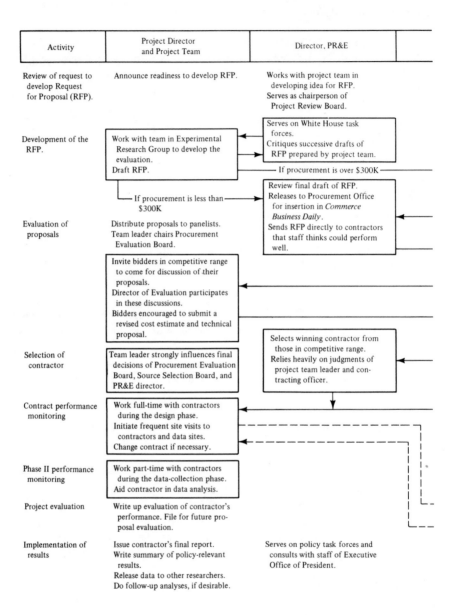

Activity	Project Director and Project Team	Director, PR&E	
Review of request to develop Request for Proposal (RFP).	Announce readiness to develop RFP.	Works with project team in developing idea for RFP. Serves as chairperson of Project Review Board.	
Development of the RFP.	Work with team in Experimental Research Group to develop the evaluation. Draft RFP.	Serves on White House task forces. Critiques successive drafts of RFP prepared by project team.	
		── If procurement is over $300K ──	
	── If procurement is less than $300K	Review final draft of RFP. Releases to Procurement Office for insertion in *Commerce Business Daily*. Sends RFP directly to contractors that staff thinks could perform well.	
Evaluation of proposals	Distribute proposals to panelists. Team leader chairs Procurement Evaluation Board.		
	Invite bidders in competitive range to come for discussion of their proposals. Director of Evaluation participates in these discussions. Bidders encouraged to submit a revised cost estimate and technical proposal.		
Selection of contractor	Team leader strongly influences final decisions of Procurement Evaluation Board, Source Selection Board, and PR&E director.	Selects winning contractor from those in competitive range. Relies heavily on judgments of project team leader and contracting officer.	
Contract performance monitoring	Work full-time with contractors during the design phase. Initiate frequent site visits to contractors and data sites. Change contract if necessary.		
Phase II performance monitoring	Work part-time with contractors during the data-collection phase. Aid contractor in data analysis.		
Project evaluation	Write up evaluation of contractor's performance. File for future proposal evaluation.		
Implementation of results	Issue contractor's final report. Write summary of policy-relevant results. Release data to other researchers. Do follow-up analyses, if desirable.	Serves on policy task forces and consults with staff of Executive Office of President.	

Figure 16-2. Program Management for Evaluation Contracts in the Research and Evaluation Method

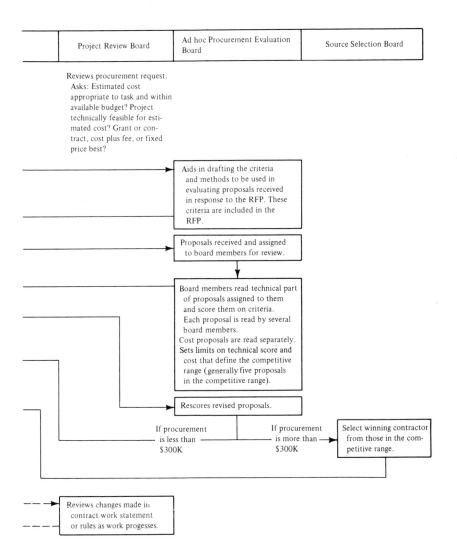

Project Review Board	Ad hoc Procurement Evaluation Board	Source Selection Board

Reviews procurement request.
Asks: Estimated cost
appropriate to task and within
available budget? Project
technically feasible for estimated cost? Grant or con-
tract, cost plus fee, or fixed
price best?

Aids in drafting the criteria
and methods to be used in
evaluating proposals received
in response to the RFP. These
criteria are included in the
RFP.

Proposals received and assigned
to board members for review.

Board members read technical part
of proposals assigned to them
and score them on criteria.
Each proposal is read by several
board members.
Cost proposals are read separately.
Sets limits on technical score and
cost that define the competitive
range (generally five proposals
in the competitive range).

Rescores revised proposals.

If procurement
is less than
$300K

If procurement
is more than
$300K

Select winning contractor
from those in the com-
petitive range.

Reviews changes made in
contract work statement
or rules as work progesses.

    2.   *The results of the planning process were models* of programs for social interventions.

B. Program Management

    1.   Project Generation: The *program models were translated into in vitro experimental and evaluation* designs. The initial design was generally done by internal staff and the final design by external contractors and grantees.

    2.   Project Selection: *Internal staff chose which projects to support* with little interaction with the extramural community.

    3.   Project Monitoring: *Projects were very closely monitored*, involving provision of technical assistance, review of progress, and coordination.

    4.   Project Utilization: *All analytical results and nonconfidential data were released to the public.* The PR&E organization did not exist long enough to develop elaborate policies and practices for implementing proved interventions.

    5.   Project Evaluation: A file was kept on the performance of contractors for use in evaluating proposals.

C. Program Evaluation

No formal program evaluation techniques were used.

**Part III
Methods for Managing
Programmatic R&D**

17 Overview

Three different methods for managing programmatic R&D are presented in this part of the book. These methods and the agencies in which they are used are the following:

Management Method	*Federal Agency*
Collaborative Research method	National Cancer Institute
Space Flight Center method	NASA/Goddard Space Flight Center
Weapon System Development method	U.S. Air Force

All these agencies are major supporters of programmatic R&D in their respective fields.

Similarities among the Methods

Each of the methods for managing programmatic R&D includes procedures for selecting a *specific end objective* for programs undertaken. The details of the procedures may vary, but the end objectives are all problem-oriented and are well specified before major R&D performance activities begin.

Another similarity is that *formal planning documents* are prepared. These documents contain a number of intermediate objectives necessary to reach the end objective and also criteria for determining whether the objectives have been attained.

A third similarity is the *sequential nature of the program development strategy*: (1) an end objective is selected; (2) a number of alternative approaches are developed; (3) these approaches are analyzed and compared; (4) the best approach (or approaches) is (are) pursued until the end objective is met; and (5) the results or finished products are implemented. A similar program development strategy is used in some of the practice-oriented R&D methods, particularly in the Research and Evaluation method.

A fourth similarity among the management methods is the *comparatively higher degree of influence over program direction* exerted by in-house staff, compared to most of the other R&D methods described. The mechanisms by which the internal staff influences program direction include (1) retaining authority to decide whether a program will proceed to the next step in the program development process and, more important, (2) determining the alternative approaches that will be developed. The in-house staffs also exert their influence (3) by developing and utilizing formal program plans to establish priorities within programs, and (4) by selecting contractors through competitive bidding to perform the planned work. The major evaluative input to the contractor selection process is provided by panels of in-house staff, with the final selection made by agency managers. Control over program substance is also enhanced by (5) close monitoring of contract performance. The techniques used include site visits, establishment of requirements for interim reports, checks against progress milestones, and technical assistance. In some of the programmatic R&D methods, in-house staff generate a large percentage of the project ideas pursued.

The degree of influence over program substance exerted by in-house staff members differs somewhat among the methods, depending on the number of these mechanisms used and the extent to which extramural personnel are involved in performing the various steps of the management process. The Goddard Space Flight Center apparently retains the most in-house control because it uses all the mechanisms and calls upon few extramural personnel in program management. Neither the National Cancer Institute (NCI) nor the Air Force use all the mechanisms. The NCI relies upon extramural personnel to a great extent in program management.

A fifth similarity is that all the methods include *techniques for supporting the utilization of R&D results.* In the NCI, R&D continues until results are proved for human use, but stops short of full dissemination of these results. In the Air Force, implementation is the responsibility of the user command, and representatives of this command and the Air Force Training Command are included in the R&D management staff. At the Goddard Space Flight Center, the R&D program management staff includes representatives of the user units of NASA who are responsible for utilization as an integral part of the R&D program planning effort. Goddard also participates in the collection and analysis of data resulting from its satellite projects.

Another similarity is that the *R&D fields in which these management methods are used are relatively well developed.* This is especially apparent when these fields are contrasted with the fields underlying some of the practice-oriented R&D methods. The management methods of NASA and the Air Force are used for programs based on physical science and technology; for the National Cancer Institute, programs are based on biological science. The knowledge base relevant to cancer—NCI's problem—is probably less well developed, and perhaps as a consequence the NCI method is less dependent on timetables and is less structured than are the other management methods for programmatic R&D.

The methods also share a similar organizational structure for program management. In all three agencies, *a task force is assembled* for each program undertaken and then is disbanded at the completion of the program. In most cases, task forces are composed of internal staff members[a] with a variety of skills, including managerial and technical competence. The combinations of the required skills differ, however, among the agencies: the Air Force requires more managerial skills; the NCI, more technical skills; and Goddard of NASA, an equal balance of both types. In the methods used by NCI and Goddard, task forces are composed largely of specialists on temporary assignment, an arrangement typically called "matrix management."

Differences among the Methods

The differences among the methods for managing programmatic R&D are fewer in number and perhaps less significant than the similarities. Some of these differences have already been mentioned. Perhaps the major difference is the degree to which *in-house staff perform the initial stages of the program development process.* In the methods used by the NCI and Goddard, internal research and management staff generate program ideas, plan programs, and create outlines for most of the major projects within each program, although there is often some interaction with extramural personnel in these activities. This provides control over program content, but requires the maintenance of an in-house staff of exceptionally high quality. In the Air Force, user commands and outside contractors generate most of the program ideas, which are developed into program plans by R&D office staff.

Chapters 18 through 20 describe in detail the methods for managing programmatic R&D.

---

[a]NCI has some task forces consisting entirely of extramural personnel.

18

Collaborative Research

History

The Collaborative Research management method is used by the NCI, one of the ten institutes of the National Institutes of Health. Like the other institutes, the NCI supports a large fundamental research program through extramural grants and manages this program according to the Dual Review method. Unlike most of the other institutes, however, the NCI also supports large programmatic efforts directed toward research on specific aspects of the cancer problem. The method that the NCI uses to manage these efforts is distinctly different from Dual Review, although it contains some of the same elements.

The NCI has not always had a large programmatic R&D effort. Before the 1960s, the NCI supported basically three kinds of research programs: extramural, intramural, and collaborative research. The extramural program was, and largely still is, a fundamental research program with awards for research, research training, and fellowship grants. The intramural research program involved direct support of investigators in the NCI's scientific laboratories to perform fundamental research for essentially the same purpose as in the extramural research program—accumulation of knowledge. The collaborative research program was used to support the intramural research program and consisted of contracts with extramural performers to provide services that intramural scientists needed in their work. Additionally, some of the collaborative effort consisted of joint projects with participation by both intramural and extramural scientists.

In the early 1960s, NCI's leadership, and particularly the director, saw a need to increase the level of effort applied directly to specific cancer diseases and clinical problems as a complement to the NCI's fundamental research programs. The NCI chose to meet this need by restructuring the way the institute's collaborative and intramural research programs were managed. Basically, two changes were made: The objectives of the collaborative research program were targeted toward solving specific cancer diseases rather than toward providing support for intramural research; and intramural research was to support the collaborative effort by generating program and project ideas and furnishing management assistance, rather than being an end in itself. Over the years, the strategy for managing collaborative research has been developed to form the management method presented in this chapter.

The NCI's entire program development strategy and organization are

145

currently undergoing a major revision in response to the passage of the National Cancer Act of 1971. The major changes will include a large program of cancer research and treatment centers and an expanded programmatic effort. The discussion of organization, program development, and management activities that follows describes, in the present tense, the NCI's methods for managing programmatic R&D in the period before these changes began on a large scale. However, much of the discussion is relevant to the way that NCI will manage programmatic R&D in the future.

Organization

The full range of current NCI activities consists of extramural fundamental research, administered by a Directorate of Extramural Activities; practice- and service-oriented clinical research, by a Directorate of General Laboratories and Clinics; and programmatic R&D, by the Directorate of Etiology, the Directorate of Chemotherapy, and the Directorate of Extramural Activities. The organization of the NCI is shown in Figure 18-1.[a]

In fiscal year 1972 the NCI operated with a staff of approximately 1400 employees and a budget of over $230 million. In that year, about 36 percent of the staff were program managers and intramural scientists, 27 percent were administrative and clerical staff, and 37 percent were research assistants and other support staff. The budget allocation was approximately 33 percent for extramural grants and training programs, 12 percent for intramural research, and 55 percent for programmatic R&D.

The directorates of Etiology and Chemotherapy are each headed by a scientific director and have a matrix organization containing branches and segments. The branches are the administrative units for intramural research activity and tend to be discipline-oriented; for example, branches in the Directorate of Etiology are Biometry, Biology, Chemistry, and Experimental Pathology. Each branch is headed by a branch chief who reports to one of several associate scientific directors. The segments are the administrative units for the programmatic R&D managed.[b] These segments tend to be problem-oriented; for example, in Etiology, some segments are Solid Tumor Viruses, Immunology, Molecular Carcinogenesis, Bioassay, and Lung Cancer. A segment is composed

---

[a]The new names for these four directorates are (in order of their introduction in this paragraph) the Division of Research Resources and Centers, the Division of Center Biology and Diagnosis, the Division of Cancer Cause and Prevention, and the Division of Cancer Treatment.

[b]The Directorate of Etiology, for example, contains the Carcinogenesis program with eight segments, the Viral Oncology program with nine segments, and the Demography program with seven.

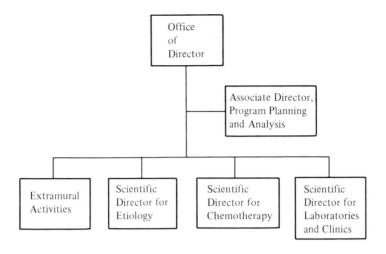

Figure 18-1.   Organization of the NCI, 1972

of from five to ten persons, each serving as program officer for several contracts. Approximately one-half are intramural scientists from the directorate
branches who serve on a part-time, temporary basis, and the remainder are
scientists from the extramural community. Ninety percent of the intramural
staff serves on at least one segment. Segments are headed by chairpersons,
most of whom are branch chiefs serving on a part-time basis. Like the branch
chiefs, the segment chairpersons report to one of the Associate Scientific
Directors of the Etiology and Chemotherapy Directorates. A detailed organizational chart of the Directorate of Etiology is shown in Figure 18-2 to illustrate all these relationships.

      A similar matrix form of program management exists in the Directorate
of General Laboratories and Clinics, except that the problem-oriented administrative units of programmatic R&D are called task forces, not segments.
As in the other NCI directorates, these task forces are composed of extramural
scientists and intramural scientists from the branches. The task forces report
to Task Force Steering Committees (one committee for each program managed), which are composed entirely of intramural scientists.

      The Extramural Activities Directorate also supports some programmatic
R&D activities by awarding large grants to nonfederal institutions. Each of
these grants is for a single programmatic effort and is managed with techniques similar to those used by the Directorate of Laboratories and Clinics,
except that the task forces are composed entirely of extramural personnel.

      There is an advisory board of nongovernmental scientists for each of
the three intramural directorates; this board reviews intramural research and

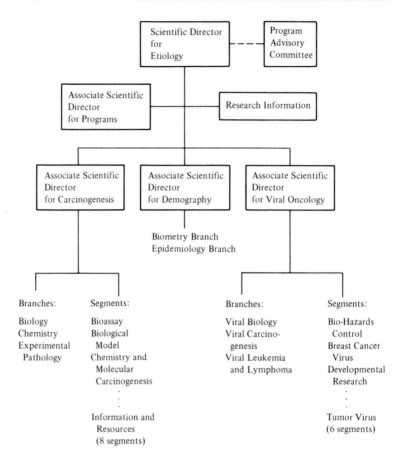

Figure 18-2. Organization of the NCI's Directorate of Etiology, 1972

programmatic R&D activities and advises the scientific director on program directions.

Program Development

In the NCI program development strategy, *a number of different R&D approaches to solving a problem are pursued simultaneously.* This policy is necessary because the knowledge base relevant to cancer is not sufficiently developed to permit a single-focus, highly programmed approach. As a result, the NCI's programmatic R&D is more expository and places more emphasis on research than does the hardware-oriented programmatic R&D method of the Goddard Space Flight Center described in Chapter 19.

To establish a direction for the R&D effort, the NCI uses a *formal framework of intermediate and end objectives* (called a "convergence chart") in managing its programmatic R&D. The purpose of the framework is to *establish priority areas* in which disease-oriented research should be supported. The areas are selected in such a way that, if supported in the proper phase, R&D activities will *converge* to the end objective of the program. The framework is used to identify and eliminate projects that do not strongly contribute to achieving the end objective, suggest new project ideas to fill in gap areas, determine an efficient order for all R&D activities, and evaluate program progress. This framework is described in more detail in the next section.

The end objective in most NCI programmatic efforts is to *develop and clinically test the treatment and/or prevention modalities for cancer diseases.* This objective does not include fully disseminating the developed modalities to practitioners.

The cancer problem is *divided along three different dimensions* in selecting end objectives for programs: by specific organs, treatment methodologies, and phases of the disease. Programs that are under way or are being planned in each of these dimensions are indicated in Figure 18-3. The substance of a project within a program may overlap considerably with the substance of projects in programs in other dimensions, but this is considered to be an important element of the program development strategy. The result is that important substantive areas are investigated simultaneously within different programmatic structures, thereby increasing the chances of finding solutions to problems in these areas.

The NCI maintains a comparatively *high degree of control over the content of R&D activities,* principally by limiting activities to selected priority areas, generating most project ideas in-house, involving in-house personnel in project selection, and closely monitoring progress on the R&D projects supported. The in-house staff are the intramural researchers in the Directorates of Etiology, Chemotherapy, and General Laboratories and Clinics.

Another element of the strategy is to maintain *large, independently managed programs of unsolicited fundamental research projects in order to provide a knowledge base for programmatic R&D.* These projects are managed with the Dual Review method by the Directorate of Extramural Activities. .

Management Activities

Although procedures for managing programs are neither uniform throughout the NCI nor stable over time, three different management methods can be identified: one for programs managed within the Directorates of Etiology and Chemotherapy; one for the Breast Cancer Research Program, which is managed within the Directorate of General Laboratories and Clinics; and one for programs supported by grants from the Directorate of Extramural Activities.

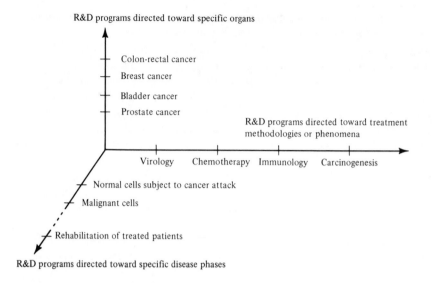

Figure 18-3. NCI's Programmatic Attack on Cancer

In the Directorate of Etiology, program management is delegated to a program manager, who is usually one of the associate scientific directors. Responsibility for managing different parts of a program is then divided among the directorate's segments. The program manager and all the members of segments included in a program constitute a *program team.*[c] Some segments manage parts of more than one program; others, only one program.

In the Directorate of General Laboratories and Clinics, a Task Force Steering Committee is formed to manage a program and is approved by the National Cancer Advisory Council. The committee then organizes a number of task forces to manage the various program parts.

As mentioned previously, in the Directorate of Extramural Activities a single grant is awarded for the direction, coordination, and daily scientific administration of the programmatic effort to be carried out at the institutional headquarters of the grantee outside the NCI. These institutions generally establish a two-tier system of task forces as in the Directorate of Laboratories and Clinics, and use basically the same management techniques as NCI.

Program Planning

Ideas for new NCI programs emerge from a variety of sources, including the

---

[c]NCI does not use a specific term for this group of managers.

initiative of NCI leadership, suggestions by the National Cancer Advisory Council, and suggestions from the extramural community.

The Bladder Cancer program, for example, began within the Cancer Advisory Council in response to evidence presented by NCI staff and others that bladder cancer incidence rates were high, and that a major programmatic efforts was feasible at the time. The council commissioned a task force of intramural and extramural scientists to prepare a program plan with the assistance of the Office of Program Planning and Analysis, and the plan was approved by the Council.

The Convergence Chart Technique

A key part of the program plan is the *convergence chart*. For most major NCI programs, convergence charts are prepared by a *planning team* and presented to the National Cancer Advisory Council for approval before monies are spent on projects within the program.

The planning team includes one NCI staff member delegated responsibility for managing the program and three to five other members—a generalist familiar with most of the research on the problem to be addressed, and specialists in relevant technical fields from either the intramural program or the extramural community. One additional member of the team is a systems analyst from the Office of Program Planning and Analysis who is experienced in the convergence chart technique.

The planning team's first task is to select an operational end objective which, if achieved, would clearly indicate completion of the program. Typically, formulating the end objective takes from one to five days.

The team's next task, performed over the next three to five weeks, is to select intermediate objectives, decision points, and steps (defined below) for the program. During this time, the systems analyst's task is to keep the team working together and to provide guidance in preparing the convergence chart.

The logic by which a convergence chart is developed is to work in reverse order from the end goal to the present state. Experience with biomedical R&D relevant to the problem suggests intermediate R&D objectives to the planning team that should be achieved in a given sequence to reach the end goal. In the terminology of the convergence chart technique, these intermediate objectives are called *phases*. A sequence of these phases might be structured as shown in Figure 18-4. From this diagram it can be inferred that completing Phase III solves the problem, but that other prior activities (Phases I and II) are required before this can be accomplished. This diagram also indicates that both Phase I and Phase II consist of two parts, each of which represents a different R&D approach to the basic task of an overall phase. These R&D approaches are suggested by the established techniques of biomedical R&D.

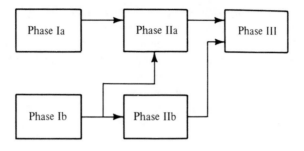

Figure 18-4. Phase Structure of a Convergence Chart

The relationships among phases in a convergence chart do not have real-time significance; i.e., phases do not specify intermediate products that must be produced by a certain time in order to proceed to the next phase, as in a PERT chart.[d] Rather, the phases specify the kinds of R&D activities (and R&D approaches) that should be supported and the order in which they should occur. The exploratory phases are supported first; phases that follow are developmental and evaluative. Activity does not shift from one phase to the next until sufficient results have been obtained.

A *program decision* is then made regarding whether adequate results have been obtained. The planning team specifies these decisions in preparing a convergence chart by selecting the minimally acceptable set of criteria that must be satisfied by the results of R&D activity in order to proceed to the next phase (see Figure 18-5).

The planning team uses these criteria to suggest data required to make a particular program decision. These data requirements, in turn, provide clues to the specific R&D activities needed within a phase. In the convergence chart technique, these activities are organized into a hierarchy of steps and project areas (see Figure 18-6).   Typical examples of steps and project areas are shown for the Breast Cancer program in Figure 18-7.

 The planning teams generally are able to be more specific about steps and project areas in the initial phases of planning; project areas in later phases are specified by program management as the program proceeds.

These steps in the convergence chart, which constitute the framework for a program, are referred to as a *linear array*. Portions of a completed linear array for the Breast Cancer program are shown in Figures 18-7 and 18-8.

The final step in developing a convergence chart is to map the project areas within the steps onto the array of directorate segments and, if necessary,

---

[d]PERT is an acronym for Program Evaluation Review Technique.

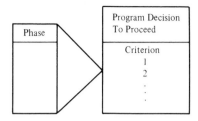

Figure 18-5. Structure of a Program Decision

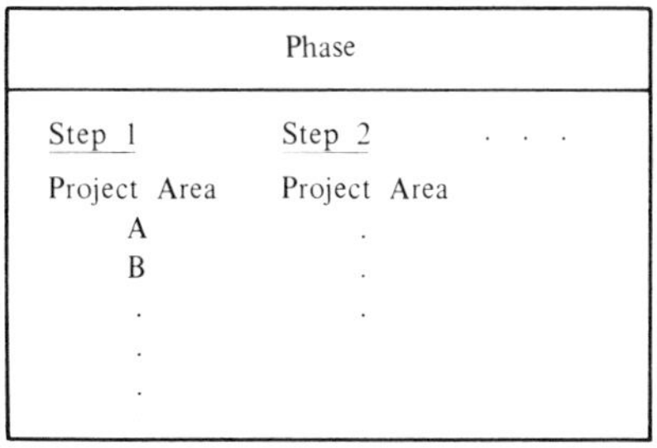

Figure 18-6. Structure of a Program Phase

specify new segments. Project areas are grouped according to the interests of the segment chairpersons and the program manager. We call these groups *program work groups.*[e]

Uses of Convergence Charts

Convergence charts are used by the work groups in the following four ways:

First, the charts are useful in *generating R&D priorities*. The charts aid in (1) assessing which phases and project areas are most important to support, based on the work group's knowledge of the problem to be solved, and (2) mapping current NCI projects onto the project areas in the chart to determine how current activities are distributed among the project areas. The gaps between needs and current activities in project areas indicate what R&D priorities should be and where more effort is needed.

---

[e]NCI does not use a specific term for these groups.

Epidemiology subflow

Phase I: Identification of population groups at different risks and general factors correlated with variation in risk

Step 1.1: Identify every newly diagnosed case of breast cancer (or breast cancer death) in large population groups classified by:

A. Geographic areas and political subdivisions
B. Race, sex, age, marital, and reproductive history
C. Country of birth
D. Socioeconomic level (via indirect measure)
E. Calendar period

Step 1.2: Examine patient characteristics in series of breast cancer cases from selected institutions for suggestive relative frequencies (e.g., high frequency in unmarried and childless women, low frequency in Mexican-Americans, high frequency in diabetics).

Step 1.3: Investigate etiological significance of preneoplastic lesions and other associated diseases.

A. Identify and compare breast cancer patients with prior benign lesions and women with similar benign lesions who subsequently did not develop cancer.
B. Follow up large populations of women with selected types of benign lesions through prospective studies (identification may be made via mammography, thermography, biopsy, palpation).
C. Follow up selected populations with disease entities with possible etiologic association to breast cancer (including effects of therapy).

Step 2: Develop case-control, familial, and pedigree studies and studies of selected population subgroups to assess relationships among factors identified in steps 1.1, 1.2, and 1.3 (including study of migrant, occupational, and religious groups, and birth cohorts).

Step 3: Investigate distribution of morphologic patterns in groups studied in previous steps.

Decision point for next step:

Select population and patient groups for additional study to determine specific etiologic relationships.

Criteria:

1. High-risk groups: a twofold relative risk (in relation to overall U.S. experience).
2. Low-risk groups: a 1-to-5 relative risk.
3. Groups with atypical age-specific incidence patterns.
4. Groups with shifts over time in incidence levels or in distribution patterns.
5. Groups with atypical distribution of morphologic types.
6. Patients with small localized cancers and with selected types of benign lesions.

Figure 18-7. Phase I of Epidemiology Subflow in the Convergence Chart for NCI's Breast Cancer Program

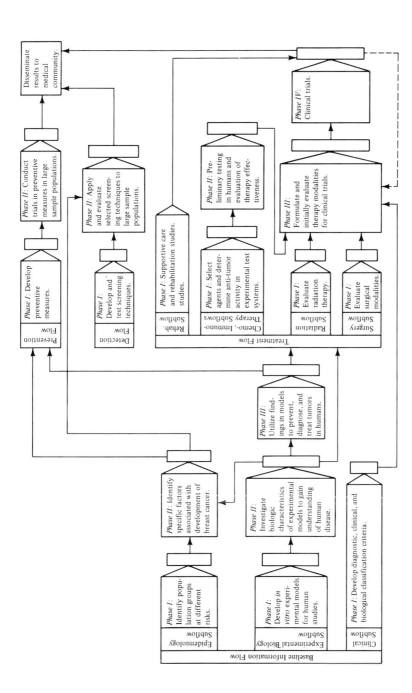

Figure 18-8. Abstracted Convergence Chart for Breast Cancer Program

Second, the charts are sent to extramural investigators along with a statement of R&D priorities as a means of *disseminating program information* and stimulating project applications in the priority areas.

The charts also are useful in *project selection,* i.e., determining which projects are relevant to program objectives. Projects that are incompatible are eliminated from the programmatic effort, even if they are of high scientific merit; however, such projects may be funded intramurally or extramurally in the extramural grants program.

Another advantage of the charts is that they provide *a program evaluation mechanism.* For example, if a number of projects supported in a particular phase are producing few results, major changes in program content may be needed. Program managers and the segment chairpersons in a directorate meet periodically (usually annually) to review convergence charts and decide if modifications are needed.

Program Management

Project Generation.   Projects are generated in different ways. Most project ideas are derived logically from the data requirements outlined on the program's convergence chart. This is done by the program work group or by the segment committees, especially during meetings held periodically for this and other program management purposes. A member of the segment committee writes up a project idea into an RFP, which is reviewed and approved by the program work group. After approval, the RFP is released for bids. Other project ideas are generated by intramural scientists who may or may not be associated with the program. These projects can be conducted either in-house, if feasible to do so, or the scientist can issue an RFP for the project and have it performed extramurally. Decisions of this type are made by the scientists' branch chief and the program work group. A third mode of project generation is to rely on unsolicited proposals from extramural investigators. Some of these proposals are stimulated by the program team. Another source of project ideas used by the NCI is an annual conference of program contractors. Often a number of new project ideas result from these conferences.

Project Selection.   A proposal received by the NCI is assigned to a segment for initial review of its technical quality.[e] The segment members convene on a regular basis to conduct these evaluations. After discussing each proposal, the individual segment members assign a numerical score between 1 and 10, signifying their judgment of the proposal's technical excellence. These scores are averaged

---

[e]In the Directorate of General Laboratories and Clinics, the proposal is sent to the appropriate task force.

to produce a *technical excellence score.* Proposals are then reviewed a second time by the program work group for "priority, need, and relevance."[f] Again, ratings are averaged to provide a *relevance score.*

The work group then recommends a set of proposals for funding, generally in the order of the "priority, need, and relevance" scores, providing that the technical excellence score exceeds an acceptable minimum. These recommendations are reviewed and approved by the associate scientific director for programs and other top-level NCI managers.

Project Monitoring. The work group next assigns a project officer to monitor each funded project. Generally these project officers are members of the segment that reviewed the proposals. A project officer typically manages three or four projects, totaling about $500,000.

Contract awards are made for one year's duration. During this time, contractors are required to submit quarterly reports on the extent of progress made toward project objectives. Several site visits per year may be conducted, and technical assistance is provided as needed.

Project Utilization. The annual conference of contractors is intended as a direct means of communicating project results to the members of a program's performing community.

Project Evaluation. The program work group meets annually to review all progress reports from projects. The work group relates the results obtained to the convergence chart, and on the basis of analysis and other considerations, prepares a statement of program priorities for the following year. The performance of individual contractors is assessed during this review, and the information produced is used in the next round of contract awards.

Project Overview. The management activities for the Collaborative Research method are illustrated in Figure 18-9.

Program Evaluation

The Program Advisory Committees of each NCI directorate meet three or four times per year to review the progress of individual programs and recommend changes. Before each meeting, the NCI staff prepares a report on programs to be reviewed and sends it to the committee members. The annual

---

[f]In the Directorate of General Laboratories and Clinics, the Task Force Steering Committees function as the program work group.

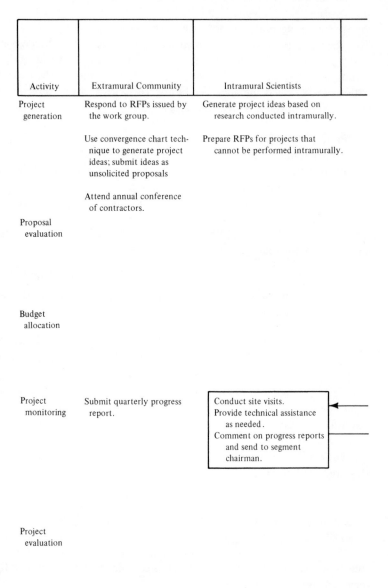

Activity	Extramural Community	Intramural Scientists
Project generation	Respond to RFPs issued by the work group. Use convergence chart technique to generate project ideas; submit ideas as unsolicited proposals Attend annual conference of contractors.	Generate project ideas based on research conducted intramurally. Prepare RFPs for projects that cannot be performed intramurally.
Proposal evaluation		
Budget allocation		
Project monitoring	Submit quarterly progress report.	Conduct site visits. Provide technical assistance as needed. Comment on progress reports and send to segment chairman.
Project evaluation		

Figure 18-9. Program Management in the Collaborative Research Method

Segments	Work Group	
Panels Approximately Half Intramural Scientists and Half Outside Researchers	Segment Chairman and Program Manager	Associate Scientific Director for Program

Meet periodically to review proposals and assess program progress. Ideas for projects sometimes emerge from these discussions.	Meet monthly to discuss progress reports, personnel problems, funding, etc. Ideas for projects sometimes emerge from these discussions. Preparation of an RFP is assigned to a staff member or a member of the work group.	
Review assigned proposals for "technical excellence." Each panel member assigns a numerical ranking to each proposal. These rankings are averaged to obtain a rating for "technical excellence."	Review proposals received for "priority, need, and relevance" to the overall program. Proposals are ranked numerically.	
	Recommend proposals for payment in order of "priority, need, and relevance" score subject to the condition that the technical excellence score is sufficiently high.	Review and approve project selection decisions.
	Assign an intramural scientist as project officer.	
	Review progress reports. Recommend changes to project officers. Synthesize progress reports and send results to project officers and contractors.	
	Meet annually to evaluate projects in terms of their objectives and to summarize overall program progress. Develop a new statement of priorites and distribute to extramural community.	

progress reviews written by the program work groups are used in preparing these reports. At the meeting, the staff makes a short presentation and then opens the discussion.

In addition, one meeting per year of the National Advisory Council is devoted to a detailed review of NCI's programmatic efforts. The format of these meetings is much the same as that of the Program Advisory Committee meetings.

Summary of Distinctive Features

The distinctive features of the Collaborative Research method are the following:

I. Organization

    A. Programs are managed by all directorates within the NCI.

    B. A matrix style of management is used with program objectives in mind: discipline-oriented branches perform intramural research, and problem-oriented segments manage extramural research.

    C. One-half of the staff of the segments is from the intramural branches; the other half consists of researchers from the extramural community.

II. Program Development

    A. *A framework of end objectives, intermediate objectives, and decision criteria is established* to guide program activities.

    B. *Several R&D approaches* to the end objective are pursued simultaneously.

    C. *R&D activities are phased* to converge to the end objective. These activities shift from exploratory modes at the beginning of a program to developmental and evaluative modes as the end objective is approached.

    D. *Fundamental research*, largely influenced by peer judgment, is also supported to provide a knowledge base for the programmatic effort.

III. Management Activities

    A. Program Planning
       1. *The framework of objectives and decision criteria is prepared before project activities are undertaken.*

2. *The framework is generated by a small interdisciplinary group* of experts working in intensive sessions lasting over a period of weeks.
3. *The framework is used throughout the lifetime of a program as an evaluative mechanism and source of R&D priorities.*

B. Program Management
    1. Project Generation: *Project ideas are generated both by extramural performers and by the program staff in response to priorities,* although the tendency is for internal sources to be used.
    2. Project Selection: Proposals are evaluated first for technical excellence by the segments and then for priority, need, and relevance by the program work group. *The work group recommends projects for support,* subject to high-level management approval.
    3. Project Monitoring: Projects are closely monitored by an intramural researcher assigned part-time as a project officer. *Quarterly progress reports* are required.
    4. Project Utilization: An annual conference of contractors is held to disseminate project results.
    5. Project Evaluation: *The program work group meets annually to evaluate the progress of contractors* and determine R&D priorities for the following year. The results of these performance reviews are used in evaluating subsequent proposals.

C. Program Evaluation
    Programs are reviewed annually by the Program Advisory Committees of each directorate and by the National Advisory Cancer Council.

19 Space Flight Center Method

History

The Goddard Space Flight Center is one of the major R&D facilities of the National Aeronautics and Space Administration (NASA). An outgrowth of the NACA (National Advisory Committee for Aeronautics) Laboratories, which conducted primarily fundamental research in the field of aeronautics, NASA was created in response to the Sputnik challenge of 1957 to build the nation's competency in aerospace and aeronautics.

Initially, NASA performed its mission intramurally by building and strengthening the traditional methods of NACA laboratories. NASA managers soon realized, however, that the expertise of universities and industry would be needed to meet their challenge. As a result, an extramural R&D program was added to the NASA organization to build and utilize this extramural community. At first the intramural laboratories and the new extramural component operated completely independently.

Goddard was created in 1959 as the first NASA center devoted exclusively to space flight. Personnel were recruited from three sources: (1) Army Signal Corps laboratories specializing in meteorological programs, (2) naval research laboratories concerned with satellite launching, and (3) NACA laboratories at Lewis and Ames Research Centers. With this complement of laboratory personnel, Goddard was at first primarily a basic research organization.

Today Goddard also has a mission to develop satellites for NASA space flights. Most of Goddard's satellite development efforts are contributions to NASA's relatively large, established space programs such as the Physics and Astronomy Program, Lunar and Planetary Program, Communications Program, and Earth Observations Program, although some of Goddard's effort is devoted to initiating new activities that may lead to major NASA programs. Goddard manages about 40 of these satellite development efforts, each with a lifetime cost of between $5 million and $80 million. This activity now constitutes about 60 percent of Goddard's extramural budget; the other 40 percent is largely for operating a worldwide network of facilities for satellite tracking and data acquisition.

One of the most significant innovations in Goddard's management practices has been the integration of the intramural fundamental research laboratories and the satellite development effort into a matrix organization. Originally, the satellite development effort was managed independently from the intramural programs, as in all other NASA facilities. But as the satellite development effort grew, Goddard management began to realize that results could not be accomplished quickly and competently without direct access to an in-house technical staff. The natural solution was to integrate the intramural research and satellite development efforts. The method of integration chosen was matrix organization: intramural researchers worked part-time on their own research projects and part-time on a satellite development effort as contributors, managers, or technical consultants.

The matrix organization provided a number of advantages. First, satellite development programs could obtain better technical advice on problems more quickly by using in-house staff as advisors than outside consultants, because the latter were in the conflict-of-interest situation of working for a company (or university laboratory) that depended on NASA contracts for its livelihood. Second, Goddard found that it could not help contractors solve problems when they got into difficulty unless it had been doing technical work on or closely related to the contractor's project. This meant that, at a minimum, some of the intramural staff needed to be doing satellite development work in cooperation with the extramural program. Third, the in-house research staff could accumulate knowledge of the state of the art that was difficult to obtain from any outside sources for use in program management. There were two reasons for this: firms were developing their own experience and knowledge individually and keeping it confidential, and differences in terminology among firms made synthesis and interchange of information difficult. Fourth, NASA wanted to control the direction of the nation's space effort and could not easily do so if the problem formulation and early stages of project design, which require a heavy research input, were performed externally. The choice was either to provide outside firms with funds for R&D and control the expenditure of this money, or to perform these stages of program development in-house. NASA and Goddard chose the latter strategy.

Organization

Goddard found that diversity in their matrix organization was essential to success. The intramural staff must be large enough to cover both the current and the possible long-range program interests of the organization. Goddard management claims that the advantages of matrix management are lost if the range of competencies available is limited strictly to current program interests, or if long-range program interests are narrowly defined. Evidence that diversity has been achieved in Goddard can be seen in the size of its intramural staff, which numbers over 3000 out of a total staff of approximately 4000.

The organizational arrangement of Goddard is shown in Figure 19-1. There are five main directorates for satellite development: the *Directorate of Space*

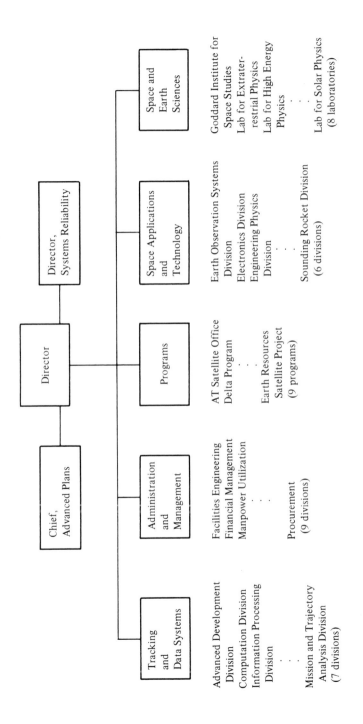

Figure 19-1. Organization of NASA's Goddard Flight Center

and Earth Sciences, which conducts fundamental research; the *Directorate of Space Applications and Technology,* engineering; the *Directorate of Administration,* administrative support; the *Directorate of Tracking and Data Systems,* design and operation of data collection activities; and the *Directorate of Programs.*[a] There is also a Directorate of Manned Space Flight Support, but it is not directly involved in satellite development and therefore is not discussed. Intramural activities are supported in three of the technical directorates: Space and Earth Sciences, Space Applications and Technology, and Tracking and Data Systems.

The satellite development effort is organized into programs managed by both the Directorate of Programs and the Directorate of Space Applications and Technology. A typical program is designed to develop, test, and assist in the launching and utilization of one or more satellites as part of a general NASA program[b] to achieve a particular space objective. Each program lasts a finite period of time and is prescheduled to produce a given number of satellites at specific times. These satellite programs are all managed by Goddard but may be performed either in-house or extramurally. If a program is performed extramurally, it is managed by the Directorate of Programs; if performed in-house, it is managed by the Directorate of Space Applications and Technology.

The organization within programs of the Directorate of Programs is tailored to individual program needs. However, some of the principles of program organization used are uniform, and can be illustrated by describing a typical space flight program.

In general, a program is supervised internally by a *program manager* who is assisted by several "systems-level" managers: a spacecraft manager, an experiment manager, a group operations manager, a mission operations manager, and a launch vehicle manager. Each of these managers is supported by a management and technical staff at the subsystem level (usually between 20 and 50 people).

The principles of matrix operation usually are applied in staffing a program. The program manager and some of the system managers are generally professionals permanently assigned to the Directorate of Programs. The other system managers are transferred from other Goddard directorates for the duration of the program, and most are moved to the program office for the purpose. Many return to their original directorates at the completion of the program. The subsystem management and technical staff are assembled similarly. A staffing chart for a typical space flight project is shown in Figure 19-2.

---

[a]Goddard actually uses the term "projects" instead of programs. In this report, Goddard's "projects" are referred to as "programs," since typically they involve an expenditure of several million dollars and multiple units of work activity, in the form of either contracts with extramural performers of in-house projects.

[b]Other NASA centers may also contribute satellites to the overall NASA program and be involved in data collection and analysis.

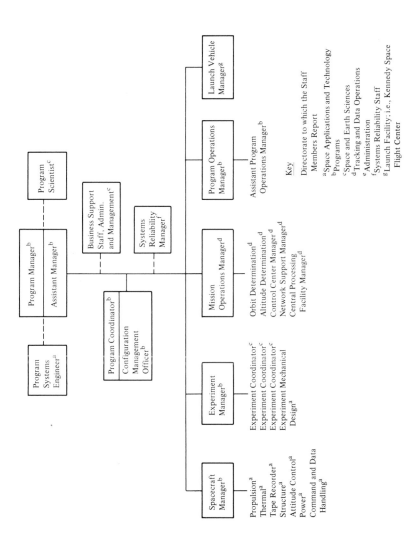

Figure 19-2. Matrix Organization for a Typical Goddard Flight Program

Program managers may be selected from one of three sources: (1) program managers of terminating programs, (2) other Goddard managers with high technical competence in the important areas of the program, or (3) the manager of the planning effort for the program. The primary criterion for the selection of the program manager is technical competence, although this does not necessarily have to be directly relevant to the program. Goddard's general policy is that if the program manager is competent in areas other than the crucial technical areas of the program, then the assistant manager must be able to substitute in those areas.

Program managers may or may not have formal management education and training, but invariably will have had some management experience. Goddard has developed a program management simulation exercise called GREMEX,[1] which the program managers and the other program staffs can use to learn management skills.

Program Development

Goddard's program development strategy is primarily based on a phased approach to program planning and program management. In Goddard's terminology, these phases are as follows:

Phase A: Study planning; generation of alternative approaches.
Phase B: Analysis of alternative approaches.
Phase C: Specification of system design for preferred alternative(s).
Phase D: Acquisition of the preferred system.

Phases A and B are equivalent to program planning as defined in this report with Phases C and D corresponding to program management. Phase C is roughly equivalent to project generation. At the end of each phase, the program is evaluated and approved for further development. The evaluation includes such criteria as

Timing: Is the time ripe to obtain Congressional and Executive Branch support for the project mission?
Staffing requirements: Does Goddard possess the necessary staff resources to initiate and manage the required effort?
Attractiveness: Does the potential project complement the Goddard portfolio? Will it maintain diversity and capitalize on Goddard's assets?

Historically, passage through all four phases of project development has taken an average of approximately seven years, with a large amount of time consumed by the decision processes between phases.

It is clear from the description of the phases that the program development process proceeds through essentially the same steps as the program development process in OEO: an idea generation stage, formulation of alternative program models, and experimentation (system design). This sequential process is also apparent, though less refined, in the Regional Research Fund method and the Special Research Programs method, where an intensive program planning phase precedes actual program management.

Another important feature of Goddard's program development process is that essentially all program ideas are generated by the intramural staff or by staff from NASA headquarters. Staff members are encouraged to propose basic ideas for programs, and laboratory or division managers have authority to allocate staff time for exploring each feasible idea. The ideas may be for a program related to one of NASA's large programs, such as the Lunar and Planetary Program, or for a program that is entirely new. These study efforts are prior to Phase A of the program development sequence.

Another Goddard program development policy is to provide the intramural directorates (Space Applications and Technology, and Space and Earth Sciences) with funds to conduct in-house research that staff members wish to pursue. This research is a means of building the organization's technical competence and also aids in attracting new research talent.

Program managers are also given funds to procure research related to their projects and to select either intramural or extramural performers. The funds are intended both for solving problems encountered in conducting programs and for attracting intramural researchers to work on the program's mission-oriented problems, and eventually, program management.

The research funds awarded to the directorates and to the program managers in an average year amount to 10 percent of Goddard's total budget, or approximately $50 million per year. This is a large amount compared to the size of the intramural staff.

Management Activities

Management procedures in Goddard (and in NASA as well) are much more formal than those in the other R&D management methods. One reason for this is the combination of the large amount of money involved in each project award and the use of competitive procurement. Both of these factors increase the need for accountability provided by formal procedures. Other reasons include the extreme complexity of Goddard's programs, which usually entail many subsystems and logistics requirements and the elaborate technical specifications required for each subsystem. Such complexity increases the need for a structured managerial environment to cope with extensive coordination problems. The general discussion of management activities that follows has been abstracted from a series of management regulations established by Goddard.

Program Planning

NASA's annual review of its overall objectives, encompassing all NASA centers, provides the central guidelines for determining Goddard's priorities among programs. Goddard has made some attempts at long-range planning in the past, but time and resources have limited it to short-range, annual planning. These short-range program plans are prepared by study groups consisting of key scientists within Goddard who make recommendations to the Goddard Management Council.[c] The council reviews and approves the program plans and distributes them to center management.

The planning of individual programs begins with pre-Phase A activity—the exploration of basic program ideas mentioned. If the level of effort required to explore a program idea is less than two man-years, the investigator obtains approval to conduct a pre-Phase A study from the branch or division chief. Otherwise, the approval of the head of the investigator's directorate is required. If at the end of the pre-Phase A study the investigator determines that the idea is worth developing, then a Phase A Program Plan must be prepared. This plan, which is typically three to eight pages in length, is required to include a statement of the scientific, technological, or operational objectives, an outline of the approaches to be examined, and a work plan and budget (for Phase A activity). The plan must also include recommendations for a study manager, a study scientist, and a tracking and data study scientist. All Phase A Program Plans must be submitted to the Goddard Management Council for review. The center director then decides whether Phase A will be initiated.

Approval to conduct Phase A activity is followed by the appointment of a study manager (generally the originator of the program idea) and the initial program team. This program team continues, with few staff changes, through all four phases of a program. The overall purpose of Phase A activity is to *identify alternative approaches* to the proposed program. The team is required to:

Develop a concise statement of program objectives
Sketch alternative design approaches
Perform trade-off analysis
Develop general plans for implementation
Assess feasibility and desirability of further work
Define relationships to other programs

Phase A activity typically requires three to six months and is conducted intramurally. The result is an analytical report that fulfills the requirements just

----

[c]The Management Council is made up of the center director and the heads of all the directorates.

listed. The team may make a recommendation to terminate the program, initiate further study, or initiate Phase B. The Phase A analytical reports are reviewed by the Management Council, and the center director recommends whether to proceed with Phase B. About ten projects per year receive the director's approval.

The first step in Phase B is preparation of a Phase B Program Plan based on the results of the Phase A analytical study. Phase B plans, which are typically 20 to 30 pages in length, are reviewed by the center director and then forwarded to NASA headquarters for final approval. This approval is required because of the level of effort involved (usually from 6 to 12 months time and a staff of between 10 and 50 persons).

The purposes of Phase B activity are (1) *to obtain sufficient information on the alternative systems approaches* identified in Phase A to select the approaches that are most promising and should be translated into systems designs, and (2) to *identify the principal state-of-the-art constraints* in each approach. Often more than one approach is found to be sufficiently promising to develop through the design stage. The study team is required to:

Refine the selected alternative approaches
Develop preliminary design specifications
Define support requirements
Assess preliminary fabrication and test requirements
Identify critical advanced technology and development tasks and develop a plan for accomplishment
Estimate costs and schedules for the total program
Prepare a work force and procurement plan
Perform comprehensive trade-off analysis of alternative approaches

Phase B is performed intramurally, although supporting studies may be procured from contractors. Some R&D may be done, usually in-house, to resolve major technical uncertainties that are critical in determining which systems approach is best. The result of Phase B is an analytical report and a Phase C Program Plan, including a recommendation as to which systems approaches should be developed to the design stage.

Program Management

The Phase C Program Plan is reviewed and must be approved by the center director and the Goddard Management Council.

The purpose of Phase C is to prepare a *detailed system design* for the technical approaches selected, including performing the necessary R&D to *resolve technical uncertainty and prove the feasibility of the designs.* The results expected of the Phase C design effort are:

Detailed engineering designs for each approach
Initiation and completion of the necessary R&D studies to resolve technical uncertainties
Final trade-off analysis and selection of the preferred design
Detailed development of subsystem specifications
Selection of payload
Definition of support requirements
Estimation of cost and schedules
Refinement of management and procurement approaches

Phase C is generally performed with extramural contracts, although it may be performed in-house if management determines that the program would contribute significantly to Goddard's technical diversity and that sufficient resources are available for effective performance. Typically, two to three years are required. The result of Phase C is an analytical report and a Phase D (Acquisition) Program Plan.

The review procedure for the Phase D Program Plan is similar to that for Phase C, except that it must be approved by the NASA program administrator.

The purpose of Phase D is to implement the Phase C design. The activities are:

Final subsystem design
Fabrication
Component integration
Testing
Launching
Operation
Evaluation of results
Distribution of results

Contractor Selection. Procedures for the evaluation of external proposals for Goddard contracts are well defined and vary according to different activity phases. Procedures have been established for each phase regarding (1) number of contracts that can be written, (2) nature of contract competition, (3) type of contract, (4) use of RFPs, and (5) responsibility for contractor selection (illustrated in Table 19-1). Except for some instances of Phase A work awarded on a noncompetitive basis by Goddard contracting officers, all work contracts require standard RFP procedures and are reviewed for evaluation by a formal Source Evaluation Board (SEB) constituted separately for each project over $1 million.

Members of the SEB include Goddard personnel, representatives of NASA headquarters, and occasionally government consultants. No representatives of potential industrial contractors are included. Prior to the distribution of RFPs,

Table 19-1
Summary of Contracting Procedures

Procedure	Phase A: Preliminary Analysis	Phase B: Definition	Phase C: Design	Phase D: Development/Operation
1. Number of contracts	Individual study contracts are written for each study area.	Individual study contracts are written for each study area.	Two or more contracts.	One contract.
2. Competition	Open competition based on scientific and technical competence in the particular study area (or noncompetitive, including unsolicited proposals).	Open competition (unless noncompetitive justified).	Open competition restricted to contractors with capability to perform Phase D.	Restricted to Phase C contractors (except for unusual cases).
3. Type of contract	*Fixed price:* where costs can be realistically estimated. *Cost plus fixed fee:* where costs cannot be realistically estimated. *Funding levels:* a. Amounts depending on contractor's needs. b. Equally funded contracts where expected costs and experience warrant.	*Cost plus fixed fee:* where costs cannot be realistically estimated. *Fixed price:* where costs can be realistically estimated. *Funding levels:* a. Amounts depending on contractor's needs. b. Equally funded.	*Cost plus fixed fee:* for large contracts where costs cannot be realistically estimated. *Incentive:* Phase D contract is a motivating factor for contractors. *Funding levels:* a. Amounts depending on contractor's needs. b. Equally funded.	*Incentive types* which best reflect level of project definition, reasonable risk assumption, and government's objectives. Experience has shown the cost-plus-incentive-fee form to be most suitable.
4. Requests for proposals (RFP)	RFP issued where appropriate (may be noncompetitive, including unsolicited proposals).	RFP issued.	RFP issued.	Request revised contractor proposal.
5. Contractor selection	Contracting officer selection (unless SEB[a] required).	Source Evaluation Board (SEB).	Use of Phase B SEB desirable.	Use of Phase C SEB desirable.

[a]Source Evaluation Board

the SEB prepares a list of criteria by which all proposals will be evaluated. When proposals are received in response to the RFPs, they are given to two separate committees of the SEB, the Technical Committee and the Business Management Committee: the former evaluates the technical aspects of a proposal; the latter, the management and cost aspects. The committees use a complex rating system and conduct their reviews independently so that neither committee knows how any single proposal is rated by the other. Findings of the committees are presented to the SEB, which, in turn, submits its own evaluations to a Selection Official who has final authority to make selection decisions. If the cost of the project is over $5 million, the NASA program administrator generally serves as Selection Official. For projects that cost less, authorization for selection rests with the Goddard directors.

Depending on practical and funding limitations, contracts for Phases A through C may be awarded to several contractors for alternative approaches, and may involve either equal or unequal amounts of funding. Unequal amounts may be awarded because of differing competitive cost positions, or different amounts of work needed to be performed.

For Phase B work, Goddard may allow contractors to submit proposals on either one of the approaches to be studied or all approaches. If there appears to be a lack of contractors capable of performing studies on all approaches, Goddard contracting officers will probably choose the first alternative. Otherwise, the second approach is used. For both Phase A and Phase B work, contracts are either "fixed price" or "cost plus fixed price."

Generally two, and sometimes more, contractors are selected for Phase C work. Only those contractors capable of performing through Phase D are considered eligible for Phase C contract awards because, in most instances, one of the contractors engaged in the Phase C activity will be selected for the Phase D award. Various types of incentive contracts are used for Phase C and D work, though some cost-plus-fixed-fee contracts have been used. Preferably, the same SEB personnel will be used for Phase C and D evaluations. Often project management personnel are used as consultants to the SEB during the evaluation, and sometimes selected members of the project management staff serve as voting members of the SEB.

Project Monitoring. Individual Phase C and D projects, whether performed by a contractor or intramurally, are very closely monitored. During Phase C and D activities, project managers prepare monthly reviews comparing the technical performance, cost, and staff requirements currently estimated with milestones indicated in the Phase C Program Plans. Summaries of these monthly reviews are combined from all projects within a program and are reviewed by the Goddard Management Council and NASA program administrator. Strong corrective action is taken when a project begins to fail consistently in achieving preestablished milestones.

Project Utilization. The launching, operation, and utilization of a developed satellite are included in the Program Plan. Goddard is in the unusual position of being an R&D agency that has a single user of its R&D products (NASA). All the other R&D agencies described in this report have a number of users, which complicates the utilization task.

Project Evaluation. The managerial procedure for monitoring progress on projects against milestones provides evaluative information on the capabilities of contractors. Records of performance are kept for future reference when selecting contractors.

Process Overview. Goddard management activities are shown in Figure 19-3.

Program Evaluation

The "system reliability" staff, which is included in each program, reports directly to the center director. This staff provides an important program evaluation mechanism that is not present in any of the previously discussed management methods. The function of this staff is to control quality, develop appropriate tests of system reliability and performance, and conduct those tests when the system has been constructed and finished. Formal procedures for evaluation of programs by outsiders have not been established, although scientific and technical panels of outsiders are convened periodically to advise the center director on program issues.

Summary of Distinctive Features

The distinctive features of the Goddard management method are the following:

I. Organization

   A matrix form of organization is used: individual extramural programs are managed and to some extent performed by a team composed of in-house researchers and engineers.

II. Program Development

   A. A phased approach to program development is used with formal decisions to proceed made between phases. Each phase provides

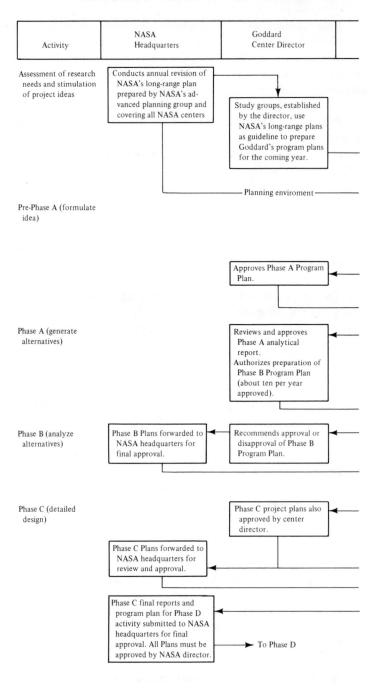

Figure 19-3. Management Activities at NASA/Goddard

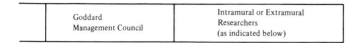

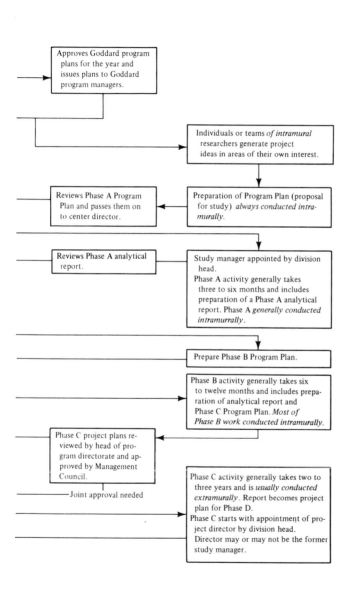

increasingly refined specifications for implementing the basic program idea.

B. The first phase is the generation of alternative approaches; the second phase, analysis of the merits of these alternative approaches; the third, translation of the best approach into detailed system designs; and the last phase, implementation of the best design.

III. Management Activities

A. Program Planning
   1. For the most part, *basic ideas for programs are generated by intra-mural researchers and engineers.* Resources are provided to these individuals for preliminary exploration of their ideas.
   2. Before performing each phase of program development, the *program management team prepares a specific plan of work* for the phase.
   3. These plans are the basis for the decisions to proceed and must be reviewed and approved by Goddard and NASA management.
   4. *Programs are planned almost entirely by the (in-house) program management team.*

B. Program Management
   1. Project Generation: Individual projects within a program are specified by the program management team and are performed either intramurally or extramurally under contract.
   2. Contractor Selection: A *Source Evaluation Board,* composed primarily of in-house technical and management staff, reviews and rates all proposals within a program using predetermined criteria. A different SEB is used for each program.
   3. Project Monitoring: *Projects are closely monitored.* Progress is evaluated monthly in terms of predetermined milestones. Corrective action is taken when a project begins falling too far behind.
   4. Project Evaluation: A contractor's record of meeting project milestones provides performance evaluation.
   5. Project Utilization: A utilization plan is included in the program plan and executed as the final phase of activity.

C. Program Evaluation
   Each system developed must be subjected to a series of performance and reliability tests before it is used. These tests are designed and conducted by a separate organizational unit reporting directly to the center director.

20

Weapon System Development Method

History and Organization

Air Force RDT&E programs[a] are often so large, in both budget and complexity, that they require their own individual systems for planning, contract selection, and contract management. Temporary management organizations and procedures are often program-specific—developed, executed, and disbanded within the lifetime of the program. Management systems for RDT&E programs are highly complex and in most cases highly formalized.

A detailed and complete description of the entire process of program planning and management for any of the armed services is not possible here. Consequently, this chapter will describe only the major and distinctive features of the managerial procedures used by the Air Force throughout most of the last decade in developing major systems, and particularly those techniques used for program initiation and control.[b]

In July of 1971, the Air Force issued a new regulation for program management (AFR 800-2) that superseded many of the procedural requirements used in the past and attempted to reduce formal management and review activities. The new regulation delegated more responsibility for systems acquisition management to individual program managers in the Air Force Systems Command, where most RDT&E programs are housed, and minimized interference with such programs by Air Force staffs at higher levels, apart from their formal review and approval actions. Comparisons between past practices and this new management system will be made throughout the description of Air Force procedures.

Program Development

The Air Force's program development strategy consists of three phases, each ending with a requirement of approval by the Office of Secretary of Defense (OSD) for continuation to the next phase. The *Conceptual Phase* is

---

[a]Research, Development, Test, and Evaluation—but excluding production and procurement.

[b]More complete descriptions and documentation of the flow of decisions may be found in Air Force regulations AFR 57-1, AFR 375, and AFR 800 series.

179

an initial period when a need perceived by any of the Air Force commands or a technological opportunity recognized by any of the Air Force R&D laboratories is analyzed through comprehensive studies and experimental hardware development to determine the technical, military, and economic bases for proceeding with a developmental effort. The results of the conceptual phase are alternative systems concepts, including estimated operational availability, project schedule, procurement, cost, and support characteristics; analysis of the threat or requirement against which they are directed; and planning documents, which are required for OSD approval to proceed with the next phase. The *Validation Phase* includes the establishment of an office—formerly called a "Systems Project Office" and now called a "Program Office"—to manage the proposed development program. In this period major program characteristics are refined through extensive analyses, hardware development, tests, and evaluations. The objective in this phase is to validate the major design choice alternatives, resolve technical uncertainties, and provide the basis for OSD approval for proceeding to the next phase. In the *Development Phase*, the basic systems concept selected in the Validation Phase is developed into detailed engineering specifications, prototype models are constructed, and plans are produced for a procurement program. All the necessary developmental work is performed by contractors under the close management of the program office.

Program offices are established, one for each major development program, as temporary organizations that exist only during the development and procurement lifetime of a program. Once the system under development is produced and operational, this organization is disbanded. Program office staff size ranges from about 50 people, as in the contemporary Maverick and SRAM missile development projects, to as many as 450 persons, as in the Minuteman missile development project. An organizational structure for program offices is generally of the form illustrated in Figure 20-1.

Most program offices contain a mixture of military and civilian personnel. In the past, high turnover of program managers and their staffs sometimes led to inefficiency in the management of programs, but recently the Air Force has extended the tour of duty of program managers and intends to include more civilian employees in the program office. Program managers are generally full colonels and above in rank who have extensive backgrounds in research and development management. They often have advanced degrees, but not necessarily in technical fields. Many are graduates of Department of Defense schools and have had some formal training in engineering and management practices.

Most program offices include user participation. These participants are usually from the Training Command, the Logistics Command, and the using command (e.g., the Strategic Air Command) and are to be responsible for setting up and using the system being developed. Users are represented early in a program to minimize unanticipated implementation obstacles and to ensure development of systems containing features required by project users.

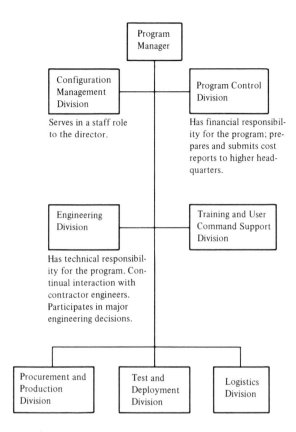

Figure 20-1. General Organization of a Program Office under Air Force Regulations

One major change in Air Force RDT&E program management contained in the new regulations issued in 1972 was the introduction of the "single program manager" concept, under which maximum authority is assigned to the individual program manager and the Air Force Systems command; and the interference of other Air Force Headquarters and command offices is minimized. In the past, all communications from a program had to go up through many layers of review and comment to reach the Air Force Chief of Staff or the OSD for a decision. With the single-manager concept, more decisions are delegated to the Air Force Systems Command and the program manager, and a *Blue Line* channel of communications is established, providing program managers of selected programs with a direct line of communication to the Air Force Chief of Staff and the Secretary of the Air Force. The many other staff offices in the command structure need be informed only after the fact.

Other major changes in new regulations issued in 1972 consisted of tightening procedures and the discipline by which decisions are made either to cancel programs or to proceed from the validation to the full-scale development phase and from the development phase to production.

Management Activities

Within Air Force headquarters, program management activities for the first two phases of weapon system development are primarily concerned with assembling program data and funding proposals for submission to Congress. After initial full-scale development funding approval, the Air Force directs its major managerial efforts toward selecting one or more contractors to design and develop the proposed system and toward monitoring their performance. Because industrial organizations often compete for Air Force project contracts and contracts usually entail a great deal of money, temporary project-specific selection groups follow detailed and formal procedures to award contracts fairly and in accordance with predefined standards. Following contract award, program management activities emphasize control.

Program Planning

Major program ideas may develop from a number of sources. Some programs start at the top as a need identified by a high-level official in the Department of Defense or in some other national security agency. Others start from the bottom, in industry or an Air Force R&D laboratory, as an application of a technological advance permitting new or improved military capabilities. Most emerge from Air Force operating commands as needs for new systems to enhance mission performance or respond to a threat identified through intelligence activities or simply arise from the need to replace equipment that is wearing out or obsolescent. The commanders of the major Air Force operating commands receive continual intelligence reports about the capabilities of potential adversaries and are provided with a host of planning documents indicating anticipated events and desired future capabilities. Some of the formal, annually revised planning documents related to the development of requirements for new systems are listed here:

Prepared by the Joint Chiefs of Staff:
    JIEP–Joint Intelligence Estimate for Planning
    JSCP–Joint Strategic Capabilities Plan (one fiscal year into the future)
    JLRSS–Joint Long-Range Strategic Study (10 to 20 years into the future)
    JSOP–Joint Strategic Objectives Plan (2 to 10 years into the future)
    JRDOD–Joint Research and Development Document (broad capabilities desired for systems and material in the period covered by JSOP, and technological accomplishments desired for the period of JLRSS)

Prepared by Air Force Headquarters:
USAF Planning Concepts—Conceptual foundations for desired capabilities.
(Prepared by the Directorate of Doctrine, Concepts, and Objectives.)
Prepared by the Air Force Systems Command:
Technology Planning Guide (Broad guidance on technologies most needed
by the Air Force).
Prepared by Operating Commands:
Objective Plans (10 to 15 year forecasts of command missions and capa-
bilities needed to perform them)

The program planning process in the Air Force is based on the *Development
Concept Paper (DCP)*, which is the vehicle for major system program decisions
made by the Secretary of Defense. The DCP contains basic program information, decision rationale, and review thresholds; and it is the instrument for
carrying out these decisions. The DCP is rewritten at the end of each program
development phase to summarize the results of that phase and to establish the
plan of program milestones and activities for the next phase. The *Program
Management Directive* (prepared by Air Force Headquarters) is the official
statement of program tasks and procedures that will be used for initiating,
approving, changing, and terminating program activities. The *Program Management Plan* (prepared by the program manager) shows the time-phased subtasks
and resources needed to complete the tasks specified in the Program Management Directive.

The planning process in the Air Force is highly structured and sequential.
The critical points in this process are at the end of each phase when the Secretary of Defense decides whether a program will proceed to the next phase,
based on information contained in the DCP and in reviews of program activities
by OSD and Air Force staff. The Secretary also receives review information
and recommendations for preferred courses of action from a committee established in the Department of Defense at the direction of the Congress to monitor
major weapons systems acquisition programs. This committee, the Defense
Systems Acquisition Review Council (DSARC), reviews program progress on a
quarterly basis, according to the milestones and criteria in the DCP; and, at the
end of a phase, it reviews the final DCP and recommends a course of action for
the next phase to the Secretary. Following approval of the DCP for each phase
by the Secretary is the issuance of RFPs, the selection of one or more contractors, and the monitoring of contract performance.

Contractor Selection

In the past, the Secretary of the Air Force appointed a Source Selection
Authority and a Source Selection Evaluation Board to choose among competing
contractors for each development RFP. These boards include representatives

of the Systems Command, the Logistics Command, and the using command. Also, in the past, a separate Source Selection Advisory Council was set up to determine the criteria to be used in rating contractor proposals. This tripartite body existed only for the period of contractor selection and was totally program-specific. The board usually had from five to ten generals and perhaps a few senior civilians, such as the Assistant Secretary. It maintained five separate committees to rank contractor proposals, each submitting independent assessments in their areas of specialty. In most cases, these committees included a Technical Committee (responsible for assessments of engineering capabilities and plans), a Management and Production Committee (for assessment of production capabilities), a Logistics Committee, a Cost Committee, and a Cost-effectiveness Committee. Committees had about 25 members each, with appropriate technical backgrounds.

The evaluation techniques used by the Air Force were designed to prevent mere comparisons of one report with another being presented to the Source Selection Authority. Instead, the techniques emphasized the development of a set of standards before proposal review and against which companies' approaches could be compared. For each of the committees mentioned, the advisory council prepared a list of items, fairly broad in scope, for which an evaluation was made on all proposals. An example of an item in the development of an aircraft would have been the cabin environment. Each of the committees further subdivided their items into factors (for instance, a factor under the item cabin environment is soundproofing), and standards were prepared for each factor. Each committee then indicated for their factors whether the companies' proposals exceeded minimum requirements, met those requirements, or failed to meet them, and assigned a corresponding score between 0 and 10. An ad hoc committee then applied the item weightings determined by the advisory council, ranked all proposals on the basis of an overall score, and briefed the Source Selection Evaluation Board and Source Selection Authority on the rankings. The Source Selection Authority then recommended contract awards and these were reviewed by the Secretary of the Air Force. (For further details, see AFR 800-2 and AFR 70-15.)

Under the new Air Force regulation AFR 800-2, most of this process has changed. The new procedures call for a single committee of 10 to 15 persons to advise the Source Selection Authority on contract proposals. This is a major policy change, the implications of which are still unknown. Although past procedures were cumbersome and costly, they did provide effective means for fair, comprehensive review of highly complex proposals for development work.

Program Management

After a contract is awarded, the full responsibility for development management is given to the program office. This office keeps in touch with the contractor (either a single primary contractor who subcontracts for required components and systems or a number of associate contractors, each of whom is responsible for a major portion of the program) and participates in the technical decisionmaking. The program office receives monthly formal progress reports and cost performance reports from contractors and maintains surveillance for compliance to Air Force regulations, with the assistance of an Air Force Plant Representative Office located at the contractor's site.

The managerial emphasis of the program office is on controlling the contractors to maintain the time schedule of development activities as detailed in the Developmental Concept Paper for initial operating capability. Program office engineers are constantly in touch with contractor engineers for these purposes. At the conclusion of flight testing and production, the program office is officially disbanded. Responsibility for the logistic support of operating systems is then assumed by the appropriate Air Logistics Center under the jurisdiction of Air Force Logistics Command.

Program Evaluation

Program evaluation is built into the Weapon System method in the progress reviews conducted at the end of each phase of program development.

Summary of Distinctive Features

The distinctive features of the Air Force management model are the following:

I. Organization
   A. A *separate formal management structure* is created for each major development project. Each structure is disbanded at the end of the program.
   B. These management structures are staffed by personnel drawn from throughout the Air Force.
   C. Some of the staff are from using commands.
II. Program Development
   A. A phased approach to program development is used with formal decisions to proceed made between phases. Each phase provides for increasingly *reduced technological uncertainty and refined specifications* for implementing the basic system idea.
   B. The first phase is analysis and experimental testing of hardware to determine alternative systems concepts and to assess the needs and rationale for the system. The second phase is validation of the

alternative systems concepts through additional studies and testing
and analysis of the merits of these alternative concepts. The third
phase is full-scale development of the preferred approach.

III. Management Activities
   A. Program Planning
      1. Ideas for programs come from three different sources: the
         operating commands as needs for weapons and support systems,
         Air Force R&D and industrial laboratories as applications of
         technological advances, or high-level government officials as
         initiatives to strengthen national security.
      2. *Program planning is highly structured*, both in process and in
         the format of documentation, *and precedes R&D activity*.
      3. *Each phase proceeds according to a "master plan"* that outlines
         major activities, decision points, and review criteria.
      4. This master plan is prepared at the end of each phase by Air
         Force staff in the program office and is reviewed by a Depart-
         ment of Defense committee and by offices in the Office of the
         Secretary.
      5. Additional plans, specifying systems designs, costs, and project
         performance schedules in detail are prepared by contractors.
   B. Program Management
      1. Contract selection: Proposal review is performed by five sep-
         arate committees, each using *predefined performance standards*
         and rating proposals with numerical scores representing the extent
         to which standards are met.
      2. *Outside reviewers of contractor proposals are rarely used.* Mem-
         bers of Source Evaluation Boards are almost always high-ranking
         Air Force officers.
      3. Project Monitoring: Management practices are guided by *formal
         regulations* concerned with all aspects of the development program,
         and compliance is a matter of military integrity. *Management
         responsibility is shared* by the sponsoring agency and the con-
         tractor, with the Air Force establishing its own management
         structure to oversee the management supplied by the contractors.
   C. Program Evaluation
      Reviews of program progress according to the milestones and criteria
      in the master program plan are conducted quarterly by the same
      Department of Defense committee that reviews the program master
      plan.

Appendix

Appendix A: Structure of Fundamental Research

Introduction

This appendix is a summary[a] of T.S. Kuhn's well-known work, *Structure of Scientific Revolutions.*[1] Among all the models of the scientific research process examined, Kuhn's was found to be the most penetrating and useful for thinking about R&D management. It describes differences between the various stages of the fundamental research process and specifies mechanisms through which scientific progress is made. With the knowledge of these factors, management can be more precise in setting conditions that promote progress and can better understand what results should be expected from fundamental research. Thus Kuhn's model provides conceptual tools that aid in thinking about what procedures to use in managing fundamental research and when to use them.

Kuhn eschews the simple model that fundamental research produces an inexorable, steady accretion of proved propositions. His evidence is that historical facts do not fit with an "accretive" model of scientific research, and that science historians are confronting growing difficulties in distinguishing the "scientific" component of past observations and beliefs from what earlier historians of science had readily labeled "error" and "superstition." The more carefully science historians study, say, Aristotelian dynamics, phlogistic chemistry, or caloric thermodynamics, the more certain they feel that once current views of nature were, as a whole, neither less scientific nor more the product of human idiosyncrasy than those current today. If out-of-date beliefs are to be called myths, then myths are still possible in scientific knowledge because the same methods used in conducting science in the past are still employed today. If out-of-date beliefs are to be called products of science, then science has included bodies of belief quite incompatible with what science holds today. Given these alternatives, the historian of science is compelled, says Kuhn, to choose the latter alternative and conclude that out-of-date theories are not in principle unscientific because they have been discarded. This choice, however, makes it difficult to see scientific research as a process of accretion alone, but also as one of revolution where past accomplishments are discarded in favor of new accomplishments.

---

[a]Any inadequacies or inaccuracies of interpretation are the authors' responsibility.

Problem-solving in Fundamental Research

The conventional model is that scientific knowledge is embodied in theories, laws, and rules, and that students learn a scientific field by learning these theories, laws, and rules. The conventional model is also that students learn to apply these fundamentals to practical cases by solving concrete problems. Kuhn asserts that this localization of the cognitive content of science is misplaced. Students do not learn laws or theories or rules in the abstract, and then how to apply them. Rather, Kuhn says, a student learns a scientific field by learning the solutions to problems. Whether a student learns laws and rules in the abstract is debatable, for even scientists, claims Kuhn, are little better than lay people at characterizing the bases of their field. The solutions that students learn are the specific examples encountered in textbooks, problems at the end of chapters, laboratory experiments, and journal publications. Kuhn calls them "exemplars." Given a new problem, students find its solution by perceiving similarities between the problems they *can* solve and the problem they *want* to solve.

After solving a number of problems, some students are able to achieve a higher skill, i.e., the ability to compose new problems that are like ones already solved, but whose solutions require a technical advance. Kuhn asserts that students never learn rules for solving problems, selecting new problems, or formulating new problems; yet with study, students gain an ability to pose new problems in their field that, when solved, are a contribution to knowledge. Kuhn calls these problems "puzzles" because of their analogous characteristics with more familiar puzzle forms.

When students attain this ability to pose and solve significant puzzles, they qualify as members of the scientific community with a speciality in the field of inquiry mastered. The process of acquiring knowledge of and the ability to extend scientific laws and concepts by learning the solutions to exemplary problems Kuhn and others call "learning by doing."

Knowledge Paradigm

Thus Kuhn argues that the set of exemplars is one of the principal elements of knowledge in a field of inquiry. Exemplars define the domain of a field of inquiry, determine the rules that govern the formulation of new problems, specify acceptable forms of solutions, and express the scientific laws that have been discovered. Exemplars function for researchers in a field of inquiry in much the same way that court decisions determine rules and law for judges practicing the common-law tradition. The exemplars are the points of agreement on fundamental entities and interactions that a scientific group requires to guide its way through the complexities of nature. It is in this sense that exemplars are a tacit expression of the state of knowledge in a scientific field of inquiry.

In addition to exemplars, Kuhn has identified three other elements of tacit knowledge for the members of a scientific community in a field of inquiry:

> *They have a shared commitment to certain beliefs*, for example, that the molecules of a gas behave like tiny elastic billiard balls or that certain kinds of equipment should be used for experimentation.
>
> *They agree on the meaning of some symbolic representations*, such as $f = ma$ (which is operationally useless to someone who has not solved Newtonian problems).
>
> *They share a set of values*, such as the appropriateness of imposing social concerns during problem formulation, the degree of simplicity demanded in theories, and tolerable margins for error in predictions.

Altogether, Kuhn calls these elements a "knowledge paradigm." Knowledge paradigms have the same relation to the scientific laws and rules in a field of inquiry as the fundamental research management methods of this book have to particular philosophies of management. Kuhn asserts that it is not difficult for researchers in a field of inquiry to reach a consensus on what the essential elements in their paradigm are, but it is usually impossible to get a consensus on what the fundamental concepts, laws, and rules are. Kuhn goes even further by suggesting that rules and laws do not exist in science, and he gives some evidence. In any case, rules and laws are not needed for scientific progress to occur. Kuhn concludes that knowledge paradigms are the basic units in the fundamental research process.

The size of a paradigm can be gauged by noting the number of researchers sharing it, which means the number who know the paradigm and use it in their work. In most cases, less than 100 researchers actively share a paradigm at any one point in time. Generally these researchers come from a variety of scientific disciplines and subdisciplines. The scientific community can be divided at the most aggregate level by categories such as natural scientists and social scientists, and at a more detailed level by discipline occupations such as physicists, chemists, astronomers, and others. At the next level, the groups can be labeled by subdisciplines: organic chemists, solid-state physicists, and so on. In most cases, there are substantially more than 100 researchers in these categories. Thus the community sharing a paradigm is usually interdisciplinary in nature; the division of scientific activity into paradigms produces groupings of scientists that intersect several of the discipline categories of scientists.

One example of a research community having a shared paradigm is the *phage* group of molecular biologists and others, which has recently been studied in the history of science literature. Another example is the group of economists who developed the general equilibrium, perfect competition paradigm. Another example of a paradigm is Newton's theory of motion. This paradigm has been replaced by another paradigm, Einstein's theory of relativity.

Using the concept of a knowledge paradigm, Kuhn then presents a model for the dynamics of the knowledge development process. His model has four phases:

Normal science
Crisis
Revolution
Preparadigm research

Each of these activities will be discussed in the remainder of this Appendix.

Normal Science

The first phase of the knowledge development process is normal science where the research activity is directed toward actualizing the promise offered by a new paradigm. Most scientists spend a great part of their lives in this pursuit. The attempt is to force nature into the preformed and relatively inflexible conceptual boxes that the paradigm provides. This is done by gathering facts that the paradigm displays as revealing, by increasing the match between fact and prediction, by amending theory, and by further articulating the paradigm to extend its scope and precision. At any time, a paradigm contains a core of "recurrent and quasi-standard illustrations" of theory and its application, but also a "penumbral" area of speculations and achievements whose status is still in doubt. An objective in normal science is to resolve these ambiguities and at the same time open up new ones for investigation. The researchers resolve these ambiguities by solving the implicit puzzles posed by the ambiguities and framed by the shared paradigm. Concurrently, however, new ambiguities arise from apparently arbitrary factors, compounded as a result of personal and historical accidents, which are always formative ingredients in normal science progress. But, normal science is inherently a narrowly construed activity. The paradigm forces researchers to investigate a part of nature in a detail and depth otherwise unimaginable. There is no attempt to probe for unexpected novelty, either conceptual or phenomenological; such a discovery could possibly upset the paradigm on which normal science depends for guidance. The game is to prove the expected. Any search for fundamental novelties is resisted. Unlike the other phases of fundamental research, normal science is cumulative in nature.

Although normal science does not aim at novelty, paradoxically, its result is almost invariably to expose anomalies between paradigm predictions and fact. Paradigms that do not reach this stage after an extended period of time are gradually dropped by the scientific community and assimilated into engineering. The paradox is that in achieving greater scope and precision with normal science activity, it becomes simultaneously easier to detect where theoretical predictions and fact are misaligned. The frequency with which simultaneous discovery occurs is testimony to the completeness of the normal science tradition and the way it prepares for change.

Crisis

Appearance of anomalies in significant number signals the onset of *crisis*, another stage in fundamental research activity. Some anomaly always exists in normal science, for that is what makes puzzle-solving a challenge. The presence of too many anomalies, however, can cause a crisis. Crisis becomes acute when the complexity of a paradigm either proliferates sufficiently to loosen the rules of normal puzzle-solving or increases faster than the paradigm's explanatory power. Crisis can also be heightened by external social pressures, as was the case near the end of the Ptolemaic system of astronomy, when difficulties with the calendar became increasingly irritating.

Response to Crisis

The responses to crisis are many and varied. The minimal response is to avoid the anomalies and work on other problems. Greater response is likely if the anomalies call a fundamental generalization of the paradigm into question, or if derivations of the paradigm are used in practice. A crisis state is marked by a turn to philosophical analysis and debate on paradigm fundamentals. Articles expressing discontent often appear. Many resist the anomalies in the belief that old methods will prove adequate to resolving the differences, and sometimes they prove to be correct. Others mount increasingly divergent theoretical and experimental attacks on the unsolved problems, exhibiting a willingness to try novelties not acceptable during normal science activity. Sometimes effort may concentrate on attacking the anomalies directly by doing research that exposes them more clearly. This activity generally results in novel discoveries unlikely to have occurred during normal science and in proposal of many radically different theories.

Result of Crisis

The final outcome of a crisis state varies, too. One outcome has already been mentioned, that the crisis is resolved by reworking the old paradigm. At other times the anomalies can be so severe that the paradigm is set aside. In this case, the researchers who shared the paradigm will migrate to other fields. Another result is that a new paradigm appears and eventually replaces the old one.

New paradigms emerge from the sequence of novel discoveries and proposals of theory that are the scientific community's response to crisis. In the past, more than a decade of crisis activity has often passed before a new paradigm emerged. Study of the atomic nucleus is probably in a crisis state at the present time, since the number of competing theories is getting larger and elucidating experiments show greater complexity than expected.

The emergence of a new paradigm is a complicated process and occurs over an extended period of time, contrary to the commonly accepted perception that scientific discoveries are traceable to a single event. Usually a "complex of observation and conceptualization, fact and assimilation to theory are inseparably linked in discovery." The awareness of anomaly, a constellation of unrelatable facts produced by the work of many people, and an array of proposals for theory are often formative ingredients in the detection of a scientific novelty. Sometimes facts and theories previously overlooked may be rediscovered. Kuhn describes the process by which a paradigm emerges by using the metaphor of a psychological experiment where subjects were given short and controlled exposure to a sequence of playing cards. All the cards in the sequence were normally figured, but some were miscolored. For example, one was a red six of spades. The subjects were not told of these anomalies. At short exposure durations, all subjects identified the cards without hesitation at their face value. As the duration of exposure was increased, some subjects began to hesitate and display awareness of anomaly. Upon further increasing the exposure, these subjects identified all the cards correctly. A few subjects, however, were never able to make the requisite adjustment of their categories, even at 40 times the average exposure needed to identify normal cards. Kuhn attributes the same set of characteristics to the emergence of a new paradigm: "previous awareness of anomaly, the gradual and simultaneous emergence of both observational and conceptual recognition, and the consequent change of paradigm categories and procedures often accompanied by resistance." Fact and theory emerge simultaneously.

Revolution

The scientific community has no calculus for determining whether to adopt an emerging paradigm (or, if it is the situation, one of several competing paradigms). Early versions of paradigms are rarely successful at solving all the anomalies which have arisen, and usually fail to solve all the problems already solved in the old paradigm. New theories usually fit data poorly, and no objective measure for goodness of fit exists to provide a basis for comparison.

Furthermore, and it is Kuhn's most difficult point to perceive, adopting a new paradigm entails a gestalt switch in the researcher's view of the world. Thus adherents to different paradigms are dealing with incommensurate entities and talk past each other on the subject of which paradigm should be used.

The gestalt switch involves more than just a change in the way a set of data is interpreted. The model that different views of the world are only different interpretations of the same data can be traced to Descartes. Kuhn asserts that this paradigm is in a state of crisis itself due to results in philosophy, psychology, linguistics, and even art history, but no alternative paradigm for explaining perception has emerged. The difficulty of rejecting Descartes' paradigm is seen in Kuhn's paradox, "that though the world does not change with a change in paradigm, the scientist afterward works in a different world." The history of science shows, according to Kuhn, that scientists measure different variables and engage in a different set of laboratory manipulations after a new paradigm is adopted. "What occurs in [adopting a new paradigm] is not fully reducible to a reinterpretation of individual and stable data . . . . Interpretative enterprise . . . can only articulate a paradigm, not correct it," where "correct" means to transform it into truth that is equivalent to nature. Paradigms are necessarily artifacts, albeit esoteric ones, that are

> . . . not corrigible by normal science at all. Instead normal science
> ultimately leads only to the recognition of anomalies and to crisis.
> And crisis is terminated, not be deliberation and interpretation, but
> by a relatively sudden and unstructured event like the gestalt switch.
> Scientists then often speak of the "scales falling from the eyes" or
> of the "lightening flash" that "inundates" a previously obscure puz-
> zle, enabling its components to be seen in a new way for the first
> time . . . . No ordinary sense of the term interpretation fits these
> flashes of intuition that are part of the paradigm-emerging process.
> Though such intuitions depend on experience, both anomalous and
> congruent, gained with the old paradigm, they are not logically or
> piecemeal linked to particular items of that experience as an inter-
> pretation would be.

Instead, large portions of that experience are gathered and transformed into a "rather different bundle of experience" and "thereafter . . . linked piecemeal to the new paradigm but not to the old."

Kuhn calls the process of rejecting an old paradigm and adopting a new one a "scientific revolution." As mentioned before, revolutions occur gradually because the new paradigm is not clearly effective in resolving the crisis and requires a fundamental, qualitative shift in perception that scientists may not easily adopt. Appeals to the esthetic may be required. Furthermore, assimila-tion often requires that some former theory and fact be abandoned, which is sometimes difficult to do. Thus, scientists do not switch rapidly to a new paradigm as it emerges.

For all these reasons, a scientific revolution is not an additive or incremental occurrence. Eventually, greater scope and precision in predicting nature will be achieved after a period of normal science activity, but a fundamental change of perception will have occurred and a different set of problems will be solved. Whether an absolute gain in knowledge is achieved is not a matter of analytic estimation.

Preparadigm Science

The usual pattern in mature science is successive transition from one paradigm to another via revolution over a decade or cycles spanning several decades. The fields normally considered to be science, such as most of the natural sciences, display this pattern.

Some fields of fundamental research have not reached this stage, particularly in the social sciences. Kuhn labels these fields as being in the *preparadigm* stage of development, a stage in which all fields of fundamental research begin.

Preparadigm research is recognizable by the existence of debate on fundamentals, and on whether the field is a science. These debates serve to define schools of thought rather than to solve problems. When the paradigm state is reached, such debate ceases. Another clue to the preparadigm condition is the absence of the puzzle-solving activity that is so crucial to normal science. Lacking in agreement on fundamentals, methodologies, and instrumentation, preparadigm scientists must always start their major expositions from a set of specified first principles. Activity is characterized by a continual competition between a number of distinct views of nature all roughly compatible with the dictates of the scientific method, but not with each other. Data gathering is more random than in the paradigm stage and more limited to the wealth of data at hand. Technology and practice (like medicine) are more likely to be sources of data, since esoteric facts may be exposed that could not be easily discovered by casual means. The transition to paradigm science has been made when specialized journals form and when lay persons can no longer keep track of progress by reading original papers.

Implications for Fundamental Research Management

Kuhn's model has several important implications for management. First, the role of exemplars in paradigm development makes the utilization of scientists, or at least scientific opinion, in project selection processes, almost imperative. The logic of Kuhn's argument is that there is no other way to maintain the integrity of normal science progress unless those making the project selection decision know the stock of solved problems. The role of exemplars also suggests strongly that in managing fundamental research, reliance should be placed on unsolicited proposals from scientists as the source of project ideas.

A second aspect of importance of Kuhn's models to management is that sudden, dramatic discoveries of practical importance will not often appear, nor will the research process respond to shifting practical priorities. The emphasis is more on the esoteric and on penetrating exploration of problems that previous research implies can be solved than on timely response to pressing practical needs. Promising approaches are pursued in great detail though they are of rather narrow concern. Progress comes in a discontinuous fashion at intervals coinciding with the occurrence of scientific revolutions. But, these happen on a scale of decades, not years, so management must be patient.

Another key implication of Kuhn's model is that disciplines are not the appropriate categories for distinguishing among scientists when placing them on panels or using their advice in other ways. A more useful categorization would be based on paradigms, since a group of scientists knowing the same paradigm yet having different disciplinary backgrounds will be able to communicate better with each other and make sounder judgments in their field than a group of individual scientists from the same discipline that adhere to different paradigms.

Appendix B: Assessment Workshops

The National Institute of Dental Research (NIDR) has devised "assessment workshops" as a means of evaluating and revising research programs. Assessment workshops are formal in procedure, but largely indirect in their effect on the research community.

Domain of a Workshop

The assessment workshop technique is intended to deal with research areas of small size. Examples of areas for which NIDR has assembled panels are "genetics of the cleft palate" and "dental amalgam" (the material used to fill teeth). Typically, there are 50 to 100 researchers throughout the world associated with these research areas. The NIDR expects that each program director will conduct one or two assessment workshops each year on research areas in her or his field of responsibility, returning to each research area about once each five years. Figure 2-1 lists the areas of responsibilities that program directors have in the NIDR.

Participants

About 15 participants are chosen by the program director to represent:

All significant approaches to the research area.
Practitioners who have a reputation for quality research on the practical derivatives of the research area.
Foreign researchers who have contributed in a major way to the research area.
Industrial researchers and developers.
Spokespersons for lines of research that the institute wants to encourage.
The senior statesmen of the research area—researchers who have been in the research area for a long time and in the past made some major contributions.

All participants must be experts in their specialty. The mix must include some who are known to hold countervailing views; all must be knowledgeable in the research area under review. The ability of participants to function harmoniously and supportively in a group session must be predetermined through observation of their performance as panelists in other panel sessions.

Format

Some of the participants are requested to submit a *state-of-the-art paper*, which achieves two objectives. First, it summarizes the current state of the art in one *research approach* to the area. Second, it states which topics within this approach should be supported in the future, based on their potential for practical and scientific results. These papers are circulated to the participants several weeks before the meeting. The authors are free to publish their works; the NIDR does not. Many of the participants prepare papers with opposing views, representing strong positions against the current lines of research.

The formal session is planned by a steering committee consisting of three consultants chosen by the program director. These consultants also serve as cochairpersons of the formal session. The consultants work with the program director and staff to select the panels, draw up the agenda for the formal session, and nominate those who will submit state-of-the-art papers. A sample research agenda from the Assessment Workshop on Dental Amalgam is as follows:

Introduction
Structure of amalgam
    Phase description and influence of composition
       on microstructure
    Influence of alloy particle size and shape
    Influence of treatment of alloy ingot
Properties
    Mechanical
    Dimensional
    Corrosive
Clinical performance
    Methods of evaluation
    Results of clinical studies
    Comparison with other materials
Recommendations for future research

The subentries in this agenda are what have been called research approaches.

The agenda generally has three phases: The first is to set down the record of research; the second to summarize, assess, and relate to current basic research activities the results of clinical research on the usefulness of practical applications of the paradigm; and the third, to discuss the best directions for research to take in the future.

Attendance at the workshop is limited to panelists and institute staff. No observers may attend.

Schedule

Assessment workshops begin with an introduction by the program director who emphasizes the purposes of the workshops, acknowledges the high caliber of the participants, and gives a briefing on meeting dynamics. The program director informs the participants that they will be asked to evaluate meeting dynamics at the end of the formal session. The introduction lasts for about one-half hour.

Four-fifths of the workshop is devoted to presentation of the state-of-the-art papers prepared by the selected participants. One paper is presented on each of the research approaches on the agenda. Each formal paper is followed by a discussion period lasting one-half hour to an hour, where opposing papers are presented, and the panelists debate informally over which topics should be pursued within the approach. During the discussion there is a strict prohibition against debating the practical usefulness of the research approach; debate is limited to scientific merit. The purpose of debate is to obtain general agreement on the current state-of-the-art and the prospects for advancement. The issue of practical usefulness is discussed later in the workshop.

The last few state-of-the-art papers deal with the clinical aspects of the research area. These papers assess the performance of the system under study in actual practice. An item of particular importance is whether performance has improved over the years. In the case of dental amalgam, the question is whether amalgam restorations last longer and are easier to install than before research started. The last state-of-the-art paper in the amalgam workshop is a comparison of dental amalgam with other restoration materials.

In the last fifth of the workshop, one of the three consultants on the steering committee presents a paper that summarizes the directions for future research that were agreed upon as a result of the meeting. A lengthy discussion period follows, during which the importance of research to practice is discussed.

Output and Desired Effects

One tangible output of the assessment workshop is a synopsis of the meeting prepared by the three-person steering committee and the program director. It is published in a top-quality dental journal. The principal requirements of this review are that it be short and written to appeal to a wide audience. Perhaps the most effective output of the workshop is the reorientation and general overview provided to the key researchers in the field.

One by-product of the workshop is the accumulation of materials useful in preparing justifications of the NIDR's budget. Another by-product is that the NIDR's efforts to recruit new disciplines into an area are legitimized and directed.

Appendix C: Quantitative Method
for Project Selection

The previous descriptions of federal agency procedures have not utilized many quantitative decisionmaking techniques, even though there exists a large body of literature on the use of such techniques in research management. The purpose of this appendix is to summarize the nature and various kinds of techniques, their current use in industry and government, and their advantages and limitations.

Overview

Most of the existing quantitative decisionmaking techniques are intended for use in project selection, which is only one of many aspects of research management processes.[a] Consequently, the methods described in this appendix cannot be considered as alternative approaches to the more comprehensive management methods described in this report. Within this limited application, however, the quantitative models can be used to help compare alternative sets of project packages and to help determine the allocation of a fixed budget for R&D projects among competing project proposals. In general, the essential features of quantitative project selection methods are the following:

Information inputs for model use are largely provided by *groups of technical advisors* who assign numerical estimates for each project (or research area) evaluated. These estimates are measures of the cost, potential benefits, likelihood of success, and expected time to completion.
These estimates are combined according to some *mathematical method* by which projects (or areas) may be compared or budgets allocated.
Using the method, calculations are made to find the *combination of projects (or areas) that maximizes* some overall index of value while satisfying an imposed constraint on total expenditures.

It must be emphasized that these quantitative methods are not intended to replace all human judgment in project selection decisionmaking. In fact, human judgment provides the basic imput of data in most project selection methods.

---

[a]Other aspects of research management are outlined in Figure 2-2. Examples are program planning, project generation, project monitoring, and so forth.

Objective data on the characteristics of most R&D projects are virtually impossible to obtain because of inherent uncertainties. Experts, however, are often able to make reasonably accurate estimates of values for these characteristics as a substitute for objective data. These values can then be combined numerically to produce overall estimates of worth. Such a technique is quantitative only because the estimates made by the experts are expressed in numerical values and because calculations are made using these values to determine optimal allocations.

Advantages and Disadvantages

A natural question, though, is why bother translating judgments into numbers at all? Why not rely on qualitative judgments? One reason for this translation is *explicitness.* When R&D projects are evaluated for project selection, there are usually *a number of characteristics,* or criteria, that are important. Some of these have already been indicated, including potential benefits, probability of success, and time to completion. In many cases these criteria may be further divided into subcriteria, resulting in a large number of aspects on which projects may be evaluated. Unless these aspects are considered separately and explicitly, there is a danger that not all the information available will be used in making the final selections. For example, in the panel review selection methods of Dual Review and Single Review, all these aspects may be considered in discussions at one time or another, but often it will not be clear what values were assigned to each of these aspects in making the final judgments. The difference between quantitative selection methods and panel review methods is that in the former, separate judgments are made of *each aspect* of a project, one at a time, and *in relation to prespecified standards;* in the latter, all aspects are discussed at once, and not necessarily in relation to prespecified standards. This difference may be especially important when the evaluation of a project on an aspect involves consideration of a complex of factors.

Another reason for translating judgments into values is *consistency.* When judgments are expressed as separate numerical values, it is possible to assign a set of weights among the various aspects considered according to their relative importance and then to apply these weights equally to all projects in determining the optimal selection. In the absence of separately valued judgments, it is difficult to consistently apply a set of weights among criteria when calculating the net worth of projects.

On the other hand, the numbers provided by quantitative methods are useful only in that they provide the final decisionmaker with a fairly consistent application of the same criteria to all candidate projects and they allow a consistent combination of all assessments to facilitate comparisons among projects. Whether the numbers are good in terms of how accurately the aspects are assessed is independent of the quantitative model and dependent instead on the competence and degree of effort exerted by the staff in generating those assessments.

The advantages of the quantitative selection method—additional objectivity through explicit treatment of many criteria and consistent combination of technical assessments—also must be balanced against the user's perceptions of *how completely* and *how accurately* the criteria conform to his or her decision framework. Indications of the quality of the investigator or institution, or complex issues of interproject relationships and balance among all the projects in an organization's R&D portfolio, often do not enter into a method, yet they are quite important to the decisionmaker.

Current Use of Quantitative Project Selection Models

Surveys on the use of quantitative models in practice conducted within the last decade have shown that, although theoretical interest in project selection methods has been high and has led to a proliferation of various methods, R&D organizations have not actually used these methods in making allocation decisions to any great extent. The first major survey published in 1964 by Baker and Pound stated: "Although the literature, interviews, and . . . data are not conclusive on the matter, it does suggest that there has been little thorough testing and only scattered use of the proposed methods."[1] The authors do mention, however, that earlier surveys by Harrel and Quinn show that "many laboratories use some sort of quantitative technique part of the time."

In late 1966, Albert Rubenstein published a second survey of theory and practice of R&D project selection which concluded:

> The practice of project selection in industry and government is dominated by . . . methods depending heavily upon individual or group judgment and using very little quantitative analysis. The use of cost and return estimates is common, but very few organizations employ any formal mathematical model for combining these estimates and generating optimal project portfolios.[2]

Rubenstein continues:

> In following the field closely since 1950, one detects very little increase in the use by operating R&D organizations of the more quantitative methods . . . . There are some clearly evident reasons for this; the complexity of many of the formulations, the requirements for data that is [sic] not generally available, the omission

from some formulations in dealing with the diverse kinds of selection decisions that arise in R&D.[3]

There are no indications in the literature that suggest that widespread use of quantitative models for decisionmaking has occurred subsequent to these surveys, nor that the problems described as reasons for their lack of general use have been solved.[4]

Three major exceptions to these general findings have been described in this book: the quantitative methods of project selection used in the OEO Research and Evaluation method, in the Goddard Space Flight Center Method, and, especially, in the Air Force Weapon System Development method. These examples indicate the practical applicability of quantitative project selection methods, at least in certain situations, even if their use has not spread to all agencies. In these three agencies, quantitative methods are used in evaluating proposals for contracts calling for large-scale, complex projects. Agencies have not used quantitative methods to as great an extent for smaller projects.

The greatest potential use of quantitative models is probably as an analytical aid in project selection decisionmaking. Quantitative models are particularly useful for examining how sensitive the net value of an R&D program is to changes in the portfolio of projects supported and for answering questions such as, How sensitive is the optimal budget allocation to changes in the relative importance of the criteria used? Which projects would be accepted if the budget were increased by some specified percentage, and which would be dropped if the budget were decreased by some percentage? In other words, these methods are used as a basis for further deliberation about the budget allocation process and for assessing the alternative impacts of changes in the total budget to be made available. In this respect, the results of the methods provide additional information inputs that make possible more sophisticated decisionmaking.

Underlying Principles for Quantitative Methods

All quantitative methods for project selection incorporate some of or all the following procedures:

Use of relative weightings of importance in combining assessments among different outcome dimensions or criteria. For example, a manager may indicate that measures of the technical merit of a proposal are equally as important as measures of its relevance to program objectives and should therefore receive equal "weight" in determining whether one project should be selected over another.
Discounting streams of income and expense to produce comparable valuations of money flows. This procedure allows a manager to account for the

usual preference that returns at the present time are more valuable than the same amount of return available at a later time.

Maximization of some criterion function subject to prespecified constraints. An example of this is maximizing the rate of return on investment, subject to the budget constraint and the constraint that no more than some specified percent of the budget can be spent on R&D in any single field.

Different kinds of quantitative methods for project selection are formulated on different combinations of these three principles. Methods based on the first concept are called *scoring methods*; those primarily based on the second concept are called *economic methods*; and those using the third concept are called *constrained optimization methods*. Each of these basic methods is described below. Combinations are frequent. For example, discounting may be used either in a scoring method or within a maximization procedure. Furthermore, different methods may be used for different purposes—the scoring method for selection among candidate projects for fundamental research, the economic method or constrained optimization method for advanced engineering or development projects. The complexity of each may vary according to the demands of the user and the complexity of the candidate projects. Each kind of quantitative method has its own underlying procedure, however, and its own set of advantages and limitations.

Scoring Methods

Scoring methods provide the simplest framework for comparative evaluation among candidate projects. Each project is rated on different criteria, with rating scores associated with different levels or ranges along the relevant criteria. For example, criterion 1 may be "probability of technical success." The assignment might be that if a project is judged to have a probability within the range 0 to 0.1 of achieving its technical objectives, it receives a score of 1 along that criterion. Extended to other ranges and criteria, this procedure produces the following illustration:

Criterion 1: probability of technical success

    Range 1:   (0.0 to 0.1)   Score 1
    Range 2:   (0.1 to 0.2)   Score 2
          ·
          ·
          ·
    Range 10: (. . . to . . .)   Score 10

Criterion 2: expected time of completion

      Range 1:   (1 month to 1 year)   Score 10
      Range 2:   (1 year to 2 years)   Score 9
         .
         .
         .
      Range 10: (. . . to . . .)   Score 1

Criterion 3:   . . .

Each criterion is then assigned a *relative weighting of importance,* which allows individual scores along separate criteria to be combined into an overall project score. If the relative weighting of criterion 1 is 2, and the relative weighting of criterion 2 is 1, this indicates that the score of a project along criterion 1 is twice as important as the score along criterion 2. If we consider only these two criteria, the total project score may be determined according to the overall formula:

Project score = (score on criterion 1) $\times$ 2 + score on criterion 2

A different formulation of the overall project score involves multiplying component scores rather than adding them. Differences resulting from these two procedures are investigated by Moore and Baker.[5]

The simplest manner of applying the scoring method approach to allocate a budget would be to compute an overall project score for each candidate project, reorder the list of candidate projects on the basis of decreasing project score, and allocate funds for the entire planning horizon to the candidate projects starting from the top of the list.[b]

Economic Methods

The second method simply discounts the expected streams of incomes and expenses for each candidate project and compares them according to their computed economic value. In the abstract, the formula is

$$\text{Project score} = \frac{\text{discounted expected income}}{\text{discounted expected expenses}}$$

---

[b]This, however, would not consider the effects of variation in project sizes and marginal returns, interactions among candidate projects, and different annual budget levels over the time horizon.

If this ratio is less than 1, this indicates that considering all the flows of income and expenses coming from a particular candidate project, the discounted economic value of the project at the time of initiation is negative. Consequently, on economic grounds, no candidate project whose project score is less than 1 should be funded. All candidate projects with scores greater than 1 represent investments of positive economic value, and the greater the score, the greater the value. Mathematically, the formula for determining this ratio is

$$\text{Project score} = \frac{\sum_{t=1}^{N} \left[I_t \cdot (1+r)^{-t} \right]}{\sum_{t=1}^{N} \left[C_t \cdot (1+r)^{-t} \right]}$$

where I_t = income (money gained or costs saved from the project in the year t)

C_t = cost of the project in the year t

r = the discount rate applied to future money

N = project lifetime, or number of years into the future used in project planning

t = year $(1, \ldots, N)$

Again, the simplest manner of applying this method would be to compute an overall project score for each candidate project, reorder the list of candidate projects on the basis of decreasing project score, and allocate funds for the entire planning horizon to candidate projects starting from the top of the list.[c]

The economic method scores candidate projects on the basis of their "present economic value" considering the flows of all future income and expenses. This same method may be rewritten in an alternative form that scores candidate projects on the basis of their rate of return per dollar invested in the project, or "internal rate of return." To calculate project scores using this alternative form, rewrite the last equation so that the ratio is preset to 1, and for each candidate project, calculate the resulting discount rate r.[d]

This form of the method can be applied in the following way. Suppose that the R&D organization that will be funding candidate projects could

---

[c]Such an application procedure would not consider any of the important aspects listed in the previous footnote.

[d]In certain cases, this method results in multiple solutions of r. Consequently, care must be taken in its application.

always reinvest its funds in the bond market at 5 percent instead of allocating its funds to candidate R&D projects. Consequently, if any candidate project has an "internal rate of return" calculated by the second form of the economic method that is less than 5 percent, this project has less economic value than simply putting the same amount of money in the bond market. Similarly, if any R&D organization establishes a minimum level for rate of return below which it wants to fund no projects, this second form of the economic method will indicate which candidate projects meet that constraint. Projects which have calculated rates of return higher than this minimum may then be funded starting from the project with the greatest rate of return.

Constrained Optimization Methods

The third basic method uses the principles of linear programming to maximize some specific criterion function subject to multiple constraints. Both the criterion and the constraints may be economic in nature or may refer to any other measure of relevance or benefit. In this method, each project is assigned a rating of either 1 or 0, depending on whether it is included in the project set to be funded or in the set to be discarded. One example of this method in the abstract is the following:

Maximize the function

$$\sum_{i=1}^{N} V_i \cdot x_i$$

subject to the constraint

$$\sum_{i=1}^{N} C_{i,t} \cdot x_i \le b_t \qquad \text{for each } t = 1, 2, \ldots, n$$

where V_i = project score or some measure for candidate project i representing the degree to which the project accomplishes the prespecified criterion (criterion may be the expected economic value, the probability of technical success, or any other R&D criterion to be maximized)

x_i = rating for candidate project i, determined by the method to be 1 if the project is selected for funding or 0 if the project is not selected for funding

$C_{i,t}$ = cost of candidate project i in year t
b_t = maximum budget for all projects in year t
N = number of candidate projects
n = number of years in time horizon for project planning

To apply this third method for project selection, choose the criterion to be maximized and score each candidate project according to the criterion. These scores are the values V_i. Supply the additional required information on candidate project costs and maximum budget levels for the future years and use the procedure of linear programming to perform the calculations. The output of the method will be a list of x_i, one for each candidate project. If the value of x_i is 1, select candidate project i for funding. If the value of x_i is 0, discard the candidate project i from consideration for the current planning period. (Again, this application procedure provides only a first-cut decision rule. Other considerations such as variation in marginal returns and interactions among projects must be considered.)

Comparison of the Three Methods

Of all three methods, only the economic method has a focus limited usually to considerations of economic value. For financial organizations and R&D institutions concerned strictly with economic gain from candidate projects, this method may be very appropriate. For most federal agencies sponsoring R&D, however, cost and economic gain are only a part of a much larger set of criteria used in project selection. In these cases, variations of the scoring method and constrained optimization method are more appropriate. The advantages of the scoring method are that it is simple and that it may not require a computer for the necessary calculations. The main advantage of the third approach is that it can handle multiple constraints and thus consider such additional complications as different budget levels for different years in the planning horizon. To show how the scoring method and constrained optimization method may be focused on *criteria other than economic ones*, an example of each is provided.

Samples of Quantitative Methods for Project Selection

PATTERN: A Scoring Method Based on Relevance

PATTERN is an acronym for Planning Assistance Through Technical Evaluation of Relevance Numbers. The output of the PATTERN method is not a list of candidate projects to be funded, but rather a form of road map indicating which technological advances are most important or cost-effective in terms of meeting various overall objectives and goals of the R&D organization. By being able to trace the relations between technological deficiencies in different areas of organizational goals, R&D managers can determine the project areas in which it would be most advantageous to invest.

The PATTERN method begins with a formulation of overall objectives provided by a planning team. These overall objectives form the top level of what is called a "relevance tree." All the lower levels contain elements which, if accomplished, would contribute to those elements above. In the Honeywell version of PATTERN, described by Sigford and Parvin,[6] the fifth level of the tree outlines various operational systems which, if built, would contribute to the accomplishment of higher missions and objectives. At the final, eighth level of the relevance tree are listed the critical technological deficiencies that must be accomplished to develop the operational systems above. Elements throughout the relevance tree are developed by a group of technical experts who discuss whether required advances are achievable in the current state of the art or are conceivable in the near future, and how objectives and subgoals would be advanced with improvements in various technological areas.

To illustrate the kinds of elements that may be considered, the following list provides samples of elements from different levels of the relevance tree used as an example in Sigford and Parvin:

Level 1: (Top Level): Overall objective   Scientific preeminence
Level 2: Subobjective   Exploration
Level 3: Context   Space
Level 4: Scope   Solar system
Level 5: Operational system   Unmanned orbiter
Level 6: Functional subsystem   Navigation
Level 7: Technology   Range and direction instruments
Level 8: Technology deficiency   Unreliability of equipment after
                                                 long shutdown in space.

After the relevance tree has been completed to relate technological deficiencies to objectives and goals, the technical group assigns relevance numbers to each element according to criteria specified for each level of the tree. According to Sigford and Parvin, example criteria at the level of operational systems may be *cost-effectiveness, political implication,* and *scientific implication,* each evaluated in terms of component characteristics. At the level of technological deficiencies, criteria used may be in terms of *feasibility* of achieving a solution, *effort* needed to solve the deficiency, and relative *subsystem performance improvement* achievable per unit of effort spent in advancing a given technology. Multiplication of all relevance numbers from any single technological deficiency up the relevance tree produces the total relevance number for the deficiency.

The output of relevance numbers can be used by R&D managers to determine the relative merits of postulated operational systems. These merits are in terms of the anticipated contributions of the systems toward overall objectives. Additionally, the relevance numbers allow managers to compare the relative merits of investing in different technological deficiencies, in terms of the importance of a deficiency in contributing toward the successful development of the postulated systems.

The PATTERN technique is a scoring method in the sense that numbers are assigned to project areas in terms of their ratings along predetermined criteria. The total relevance numbers, or total project area scores, are determined by multiplying component ratings up through the relevance tree. The main difference between the PATTERN method and the abstract scoring method presented earlier is that criteria in PATTERN are arranged hierarchically, and the weight given to any criterion is dependent on the ratings of all the elements at higher levels on the tree.

One feature provided by the PATTERN technique and usually absent in scoring methods is a way of measuring cross-project impact. Reference to the relevance tree in PATTERN will indicate to an R&D manager how advances in one area of technological deficiency will affect advances required in other areas of deficiency.

TORQUE: A Constrained Optimization Method Based on Utility of Effort

TORQUE is an acronym for Technology Or Research Quantities Utility Evaluation. The technique was developed in the late 1960s by an interservice team for the Department of Defense, and it has been tested by the Air Force as a management tool for allocating an R&D budget among alternative project areas. A more detailed description of the TORQUE method is presented by Nutt.[7]

TORQUE uses the same reasoning found in PATTERN to outline overall objectives and determine technological advances required. It goes beyond the results of PATTERN, however, in determining the level of funds which should be allocated to each area of technological deficiency in order to maximize the overall utility from all the areas funded.

Like PATTERN, TORQUE begins with a listing of overall objectives. The selection of objectives and their rankings in order of importance to the R&D organization are provided by planning teams. Other interdisciplinary teams of technical experts develop alternative approaches to realizing the objectives and identify the technological advances required. In a procedure analogous to providing relevance numbers, TORQUE planners assign ratings on the criticality of a technology area to the approach or system which it supports.

The next steps extend the scope of TORQUE into the area of resource

allocation. The first task is for the teams of technical experts to sort technological areas into related groups and divide the groups into successive levels of
difficulty. Next, the technology teams determine the resources required to
achieve the various technologies identified. The final step is to determine the
best allocation of funds in support of different Levels of Difficulty (LOD) for
each technology area.

To determine the best use of funds, the TORQUE method calculates, for
each LOD for a technology area, a utility score, defined as

$$U = \sum_{i=1}^{N} C_i \cdot W_i \cdot C_f \cdot t_i$$

where U = utility of achieving a particular LOD for a particular technology
area
N = number of systems or approaches supported by the LOD
C_i = criticality of the LOD to the ith system or approach supported
(criticality ratings range from 0 as "no contribution" to 1.0 as
"absolutely essential")
W_i = relative weight of "importance" of the ith system or approach
(in reference to the objective supported)
C_f = ratio of first-year funds allocated to the technology in which
this LOD belongs to the total funds required to achieve the technology
t_i = "timeliness function" (undefined by Nutt)

A computer program then selects, from all combinations of allocation levels for
the different technologies, the set of funding assignments that provides maximum utility for the funds available.

Overall Perspective

In using methods such as TORQUE and PATTERN, the final outcomes do
not represent uncontested decisions concerning selection of candidate projects.
In describing Honeywell's application of the PATTERN method, C.L. Davis,
Vice President of the Military Products Group, emphasized: "We are not being
managed by a computer. But the questions being tackled by Project PATTERN
in the complex area of technical relevance are those traditionally most difficult
for an R&D decision-maker to handle. Most of the others are being answered
through conventional management and marketing channels."[8]

For application of TORQUE, Nutt similarly emphasized: "TORQUE is
designed to supplement the intuition of managers at all levels by combining

expert subjective judgments in a structured fashion to serve as a tool or aid in the decisionmaking process. It is almost superfluous to add that the system is in no way intended to supplant the manager.[9]

Quantitative models of any kind that aid in the management process of project selection may be highly valuable tools. But project selection is only a small part of the total management process required in conducting programmatic R&D. Systems of organizational structure, proposal stimulation and review, and program planning and evaluation are all essential ingredients in any plan of R&D management. The descriptions of the various quantitative tools described in this appendix provide a small indication of the variety of management aids available for conducting large-scale efforts of R&D.

Appendix D: Persons Interviewed During the Preparation of this Book[a]

R. Keith Arnold
  Deputy Chief, Forestry Research
  Forest Service
  Department of Agriculture

George E. Arnstein
  Office of Government and
  Public Problems
  NSF

Betty Barton
  Chief, Scientific Conference Branch
  National Institute of Child Health
  and Human Development
  National Institutes of Health
  DHEW

Kenneth Baum
  FAST Task Force
  DHEW

William Bevan
  Executive Officer
  American Association for the
  Advancement of Science

Carl R. Brewer
  Chief, General Research
  Support Branch
  National Institutes of Health
  DHEW

Lee Burchinal
  Director, National Center for
  Educational Communications
  Office of Education
  DHEW

Michael F. Burke
  Chief, Procurement Division
  OEO

Benjamin T. Burton
  Deputy Director, National Institute
  of Arthritis and Metabolic Diseases
  National Institutes of Health
  DHEW

Louis M. Carrese
  Associate Director, Program
  Planning and Analysis
  National Cancer Institute
  National Institutes of Health
  DHEW

Herbert C. Christoferson
  Executive Officer, National Institute
  of Dental Research
  National Institutes of Health
  DHEW

Joe F. Coates
  Office of Exploratory Research and
  Problem Assessment
  Research Applied to National Needs
  NSF

---

[a]Affiliations listed are those held at the time of consultation.

George A. Comstock
  Surgeon General's Task Force on
  TV and Social Behavior
  National Institute of Mental Health
  HSMHA

Eugene A. Confrey
  Director, Bureau of Health
  Manpower Education
  National Institutes of Health
  DHEW

William V. Consolazio
  Director, Division of Institutional
  Development
  NSF

Theodore Cooper
  Director, National Heart and
  Lung Institute
  National Institures of Health
  DHEW

James D. Cowhig
  Office of Social Systems and
  Human Resources
  Research Applied to National Needs
  NSF

Howard Davis
  Chief, Mental Health Services
  Development Branch
  National Institute of Mental Health
  HSMHA

Lloyd H. Davis
  Science and Education
  Department of Agriculture

Josephine K. Doherty
  International Biology Program
  NSF

Ken L. Eaton
  Deputy Director, National Institute
  of Alcohol Abuse and Alcoholism
  National Institute of Mental Health
  HSMHA

John Egermeier
  Chief, Research Training Branch
  National Center for Education
  Research and Development
  Office of Education
  DHEW

Leon Ellwein
  Program Planning and Analysis
  National Cancer Institute
  National Institutes of Health
  DHEW

Edward J. Flynn
  Chief, Applied Research Branch
  National Institute of Mental Health
  HSMHA

Thomas O. Fontaine
  Deputy Assistant Director for
  Education
  NSF

John Gardener
  Chief, Program Staff Office
  Chief of Police Research,
  Planning, Evaluation, and
  Coordination
  National Institute of Law Enforce-
  ment and Criminal Justice
  LEAA

Clair L. Gardner
  Deputy Director, National Institute
  of Dental Research
  National Institutes of Health
  DHEW

Dorothy Gilford
Director, National Center for
Educational Statistics
Office of Education
DHEW

Thomas K. Glennan
Director, Office of Planning,
Research, and Evaluation
Office of Economic Opportunity

Wayne R. Gruner
Senior Staff Associate (Planning)
Research Directorate
NSF

Howard J. Hausman
Senior Staff Associate
Education Directorate
NSF

Karl Heresford
Director, Planning and Evaluation
Bureau of Elementary and
Secondary Education
Office of Education
DHEW

Kenneth K. Hisaoka
Director, Developmental Biology
and Oral Facial Anomalies Program
National Institute of Dental Research
National Institutes of Health
DHEW

Frank Isakson
Director, Physics Branch
Office of Naval Research
Department of the Navy

Keith R. Kelson
Executive Assistant
Education Directorate
NSF

Stephen C. King
Deputy Administrator, Livestock
Agricultural Research Service
Department of Agriculture

Seymour J. Kreshover
Director, National Institute of
Dental Research
National Institutes of Health
DHEW

R.W. Lamont Havers
Associate Director for Extramural
Research and Training
National Institutes of Health
DHEW

Leonard Laster
Office of Science and Technology
Executive Office of the President

Louis Levin
Assistant Director for Institutional
Programs
NSF

Thomas E. Malone
Associate Director for Extramural
Programs
National Institute of Dental Research
National Institutes of Health
DHEW

John McDougall
Associate Director for Program
Services
National Institute of Child Health
and Human Development
National Institutes of Health
DHEW

William A. Mecca
  Chief, Program Support Division
  Goddard Space Flight Center
  National Aeronautics and Space
  Administration

Loren R. Mosher
  Chief, Center for Study of
  Schizophrenia
  National Institute of Mental Health
  HSMHA

James Moss
  Director of Research, Bureau of the
  Handicapped
  Office of Education
  DHEW

Edwin J. Nichols
  Chief, Center for Child and Family
  Mental Health
  National Institute of Mental Health
  HSMHA

James F. O'Donnell
  Assistant Director, Division of
  Research Resources
  National Institutes of Health
  DHEW

Edward P. Offutt
  Deputy Associate Director for
  Extramural Programs
  National Institute of Arthritis and
  Metabolic Diseases
  National Institutes of Health
  DHEW

Albert A. Pawlowski
  Chief, Research Branch
  National Institute of Alcohol Abuse
  and Alcoholism
  National Institute of Mental Health
  HSMHA

Monte Penney
  Basic Research Branch
  Office of Education
  DHEW

James A. Peters
  Assistant to the Scientific
  Director for Etiology
  National Cancer Institute
  National Institutes of Health
  DHEW

Harry Phillips
  Director, Bureau State
  Agency Coordination
  Office of Education
  DHEW

Betty H. Pickett
  Deputy Director, Division
  of Extramural Research Programs
  National Institute of Mental Health
  HSMHA

Robert Pitchell
  Executive Director, National
  University Extension Association

Senta Raizen
  Special Assistant,
  Education Directorate
  NSF

Joseph E. Rall
  Director for Intramural Research
  National Institute of Arthritis and
  Metabolic Diseases
  National Institutes of Health
  DHEW

N.P. Ralston
  Associate Director, Science and
  Education
  Department of Agriculture

Lillian Reggelson
Director of Evaluation, Office of
Planning, Research, and Evaluation
OEO

John S. Robins
Deputy Administrator, Cooperative
State Research Service
Department of Agriculture

Mary Robinson
Experimental Research Division A,
Office of Planning, Research,
and Evaluation
OEO

Bertha W. Rubenstein
Social Sciences Division
NSF

S. Stephen Schiaffino
Chief, Research Grants Review
Branch
Division of Research Grants
National Institutes of Health
DHEW

Jefferey Schiller
Director, Experimental Research
Division
Office of Planning, Research,
and Evaluation
OEO

Leon Schwartz
Associate Commissioner for
Administration
Office of Education
DHEW

Richard L. Seggel
Associate Director for
Administration
National Institutes of Health
DHEW

Saleem A. Shah
Chief, Center for Studies of
Crime and Delinquency
National Institute of Mental Health
HSMHA

John F. Sherman
Deputy Director
National Institutes of Health
DHEW

Henry W. Sherp
Special Assistant to the Director
National Institute of Dental Research
National Institutes of Health
DHEW

Bernard Sisco
Assistant Director for Administration
NSF

Herbert C. Storey
Forestry Research
Forest Service
Department of Agriculture

Philip Teske
Chief, Instructional
Materials and Practices Branch
National Center for Educational
Research and Development
Office of Education
DHEW

Theodore Tjossem
Program Director, Mental
Retardation Branch
National Institute of Child Health
and Human Development
National Institutes of Health
DHEW

Mark S. Tucker
Secretary, Educational Development
Corporation

Michael J. Vaccaro
  Associate Director for Administration
  Goddard Space Flight Center
  National Aeronautics and Space
  Administration

Louis A. Wienckowski
  Director of Extramural Research
  Programs
  National Institute of Mental Health
  HSMHA

Clyde A. Williams
  Deputy Director for Program and
  Staff Development
  Extension Service
  Department of Agriculture

Gilbert Woodside
  Associate Director for Extramural
  Programs
  National Institute of Child Health
  and Human Development
  National Institutes of Health
  DHEW

Notes

Introduction

1. For details of this plan, see R.E. Levien, *A Preliminary Plan for the National Institute of Education*, The Rand Corporation, R-653-HEW, February 1971.
2. T.S. Kuhn, *The Structure of Scientific Revolutions*, International Encyclopedia of Science, Vol. 2, No. 2, University of Chicago Press, Chicago, 1970. A summary of Kuhn's work appears as Appendix A.

Chapter 2
Dual Review

1. U.S. Department of Health, Education, and Welfare, *The Division of Research Grants, Its History, Organization, and Functions, 1945-1962*, Public Health Service Publication No. 1032, Washington, D.C., March 1963.

Chapter 3
Single Review

1. U.S. Congress, National Science Foundation Act of 1950, Public Law 507, 81st Cong., 64 Stat., 149; 42 U.S.C., 1861-1875, as amended.

Chapter 5
"No" Review

1. Bruce Old, et al., "The Evolution of the Office of Naval Research," *Physics Today*, Vol. 14, No. 8, pp. 30-35, August 1961.
2. Richard Rettig, "Federal Support of Scientific Research, A Comparative Study," Unpublished Ph.D. dissertation, Massachusetts Institute of Technology, Cambridge, August 1967, p. 97.
3. Richard Rettig, *ibid.*, p. 90.
4. U.S. Office of Naval Research, *Research Management Guide*, Department of the Navy, Washington, D.C., p. II-2, undated.

Chapter 7
Management Methods of the Cooperative State Research Service

1. U.S. Department of Agriculture, *After a Hundred Years: The Yearbook of Agriculture*, U.S. Government Printing Office, Washington, D.C., 1962.

Chapter 19
Space Flight Center Method

1. For a more detailed description of GREMEX, see E.B. McGregor and R.F.
   Baker, "GREMEX—A Management Game for the New Public Administration," *Public Administration Review*, January-February 1972, pp. 24-32.

Appendix A
Structure of Fundamental Research

1. T.S. Kuhn, *Structure of Scientific Revolutions*, International Encyclopedia
   of Science, Vol. 2, No. 2, University of Chicago Press, Chicago, 1970.

Appendix C
Quantitative Methods for Project Selection

1. N.R. Baker and W.H. Pound, "R&D Project Selection: Where We Stand,"
   IEEE Transactions on Engineering Management, Vol. EM-11, December
   1964, p. 130.
2. Albert H. Rubenstein, "Economic Evaluation of Research and Development:
   A Brief Survey of Theory and Practice," *The Journal of Industrial Engineering*, Vol. 17, No. 11, November 1966, p. 616.
3. *Ibid.*, p. 616.
4. W.E. Souder, "Analytical Effectiveness of Mathematical Models for R&D
   Project Selection," *Management Science*, Vol. 19, No. 8, April 1973.
5. John R. Moore and Norman R. Baker, "Computational Analysis of Scoring
   Models for R&D Project Selection," *Management Science*, Vol. 16, No. 4,
   December 1969, pp. B212-B232.
6. J.V. Sigford and R.H. Parvin, "Project PATTERN: A Methodology for
   Determining Relevance in Complex Decision-making," *IEEE Transactions
   on Engineering Management*, Vol. EM-12, March 1965, pp. 9-13.
7. A.B. Nutt, "Testing TORQUE—A Quantitative R&D Resource-allocation
   System," *IEEE Transactions on Engineering Management*, Vol. EM-16,
   November 1969, pp. 246-248.
8. Sigford and Parvin, *op. cit.*, p. 9.
9. Nutt, *op. cit.*, p. 246.

Selected Bibliography

Association of State Universities and Land Grant Colleges and U.S. Department of Agriculture, *A National Program of Research for Agriculture*, Washington, D.C., October 1966.

Baker, N.R., and W.H. Pound, "R&D Project Selection: Where We Stand," *IEEE Transactions on Engineering Management*, Vol. EM-11, December 1964, pp. 124-134.

Barro, S.M., *An Exploratory Study of Science Resource Allocation*, The Rand Corporation, RM-5804-NSF, March 1969.

Carrese, Louis M., and Carl G. Baker, "The Convergence Technique: A Method for the Planning and Programming of Research Efforts," *Management Science*, Vol. 13, No. 8, April 1967, pp. B-420 to B-438.

Department of the Navy, Office of Naval Research, *Research Management Guide*, Washington, D.C., undated.

Glueck, William F., and Carl D. Thorp, *The Management of Scientific Research: An Annotated Bibliography and Synopsis*, Research Center, School of Business and Public Administration, University of Missouri, 1971.

Moore, John R., and Norman R. Baker, "Computational Analysis of Scoring Models for R&D Project Selection," *Management Science*, Vol. 16, No. 4, December 1969, pp. B212-B232.

Nutt, A.B., "Testing TORQUE—A Quantitive R&D Resource-allocation System," *IEEE Transactions on Engineering Management*, Vol. EM-16, November 1969, pp. 243-248.

Perl, Martin L., "The Scientific Advisory System: Some Observations," *Science*, Vol. 173, No. 4003, September 24, 1971, pp. 1211-1215.

Rettig, Richard A., "Federal Support of Scientific Research: A Comparative Study," Ph.D. dissertation, Massachusetts Institute of Technology, August 1967.

Roberts, Richard, and Roland Schmitt, "Creativity versus Planning—You CAN Have Both," *Innovation*, No. 19, March 1971, pp. 51-58.

Rosen, E.M., and William E. Souder, "A Method for Allocating R&D Expenditures," *IEEE Transactions on Engineering Management*, Vol. EM-12, September 1965, pp. 87-93.

Rosenberg, Herbert H., "Research Planning and Program Development in the National Institutes of Health: The Experience of a Relatively New and Growing Agency," *Annals of American Academy of Political and Social Science*, Vol. 327, January 1960, pp. 103-113.

Rubenstein, Albert H., "Economic Evaluation of Research and Development: A Brief Survey of Theory and Practice," *The Journal of Industrial Engineering,* Vol. XVII, No. 11, November 1966, pp. 615-620.

Rubinstein, Eli A., "The Federal Health Scientist-Administrator: An Opportunity for Role Integration," *American Psychologist,* Vol. 23, No. 8, August 1968, pp. 558-564.

Schröeder, Hans-Horst, "R&D Project Evaluation and Selection Models for Development: A Survey of the State of the Art," *Socio-Economic Planning Science,* Vol. 5, 1971 (also published by Pergamon Press, Great Britain, pp. 25-(39).

Shaffter, Dorothy, *The National Science Foundation,* Praeger Library of U.S. Government Departments and Agencies, Frederick A. Praeger, Inc., Publishers, New York, 1969.

Shaw, Byron T., "Research Planning and Control in the United States Department of Agriculture: The Experience of an Old and Well-established Research Agency," *Annals of American Academy of Political and Social Science,* Vol. 327, January 1960, pp. 95-102.

Sigford, J.V., and R.H. Parvin, "Project PATTERN: A Methodology for Determining Relevance in Complex Decision-Making," *IEEE Transactions on Engineering Management,* Vol. EM-12, March 1965, pp. 9-13.

Terselic, Richard A., and L.M. Carrese, "Monitoring Technical Progress in Research and Development Contracts," *National Contract Management Journal,* Vol. 3, No. 2, 1969, pp. 62-73.

U.S. Department of Agriculture, Cooperative State Research Service, *Manual of Procedures for Cooperative Regional Research,* CSRS-OD-1082, Washington, D.C., January 1970.

U.S. Department of Agriculture, *State Agricultural Experiment Stations, A History of Research Policy and Procedure,* Miscellaneous Publication No. 904, U.S. Government Printing Office, Washington, D.C., May 1962.

U.S. Department of Health, Education, and Welfare, Public Health Service, National Institutes of Health, *NIH Public Advisory Groups,* Washington, D.C., July 1, 1970.

U.S. Department of Health, Education, and Welfare, Public Health Service, National Institutes of Health, *Science, Public Policy and the Scientist Administrator: An Anthology,* Washington, D.C., 1970-1971.

Wade, Nicholas, "Special Virus Cancer Program: Travails of a Biological Moonshot," *Science,* Vol. 1974, December 24, 1971, pp. 1306-1311.

Index

National Advisory Mental Health
Council, 51, 88, 94, 95, 96, 109
National Aeronautics and Space Administration.
See NASA/Goddard Space Flight
Center
National Association of State Universities and Land Grant Colleges,
57, 70
National Cancer Act, 146
National Cancer Advisory Council,
150, 151, 160
National Cancer Institute (NCI), 7,
142, 143, 145-161; Divisions, 146n;
and Dual Review, 145, 149; history,
145-146; management activities,
149-160; and NASA, 148; Office
of Program Planning and Analysis,
151; organization, 146-148; program development, 148-149; Task
Force Steering Committee, 150,
157n
National Institute of Dental Research
(NIDR), 199
National Institute of Education (NIE),
xx
National Institute of Mental Health
(NIMH), 87-91; Applied Research,
88, 93-99; Centers for Alcohol
and Drug Abuse, 89, 90; Coordinating Centers, 89-90, 101-106; Extramural Research Programs, 88,
93, 94, 102; history, 87-89, 113;
management activities, 94-96, 102-
105, 108-110, 116-118; and NIH,
50, 87, 89, 90, 95; and OEO, 121;
Operating Centers, 90, 107-111;
organization, 89-91, 94, 101-102,
107, 114-115; program development, 93, 102, 107-108, 114;
Services R&D, 88-89, 113-119;
Special Mental Health Programs,
89-90, 102, 107, 113; staffing,
96
National Institutes of Health (NIH),
7-22; Division of Research Grants,
8, 10, 20, 95, 104; executive sec-

retaries, 8, 20; grants, 10-11; history, 7-8; institutes, 8-10; management activities, 11-15; and NCI,
145; and NIMH, 50, 87, 89, 90;
organization, 8-10; program development, 10-11; staffing, 15-20
National Mental Health Act, 87
National Science Board, 23, 27, 29
National Science Foundation (NSF),
history, 23; Mail Review, 33-37;
management activities, 24-28, 33-
35; and ONR, 23; organization,
23-24, 33; program development,
24, 33; Single Review, 23-32;
staffing, 28-29
"No" Review, 5, 39-45
"Normal science" (Kuhn), 24, 192-193
Nutt, A.B., 213, 214-215

OEO.
See Office of Economic Opportunity
ONR.
See Office of Naval Research
OSD.
See Office of Secretary of Defense
Office of Economic Opportunity
(OEO), 121-138; and Executive
Office of the President, 121, 123,
127, 134; General Counsel, 131,
132, 133, 134, 135; Grant and Con-
tract Review, 131, 132, 133, 134;
history, 121; management activities,
126-134, 206; and NASA, 169; and
NIMH, 121; Offices of Health Af-
fairs, Legal Services, Operations,
Program Development, 121-122; or-
ganization, 121-123; program development, 124-126; Project Review Board, 131, 133, 134; and
Regional Research Fund, 126n;
staffing, 134-135; and USDA, 121
Office of Economic Opportunity Act
(Title II), 122
Office of Naval Research (ONR), 39-
45; history, 39; management activities, 41-44; and NASA, 163;
and NSF, 23; organization, 41;

Selected List of Rand Books

Bagdikian, Ben H. *The Information Machines: Their Impact on Men and the Media*. New York: Harper and Row, 1971.

Canby, Steven L. *Military Manpower Procurement: A Policy Analysis*. Lexington, Mass.: Lexington Books, D.C. Heath and Company, Inc., 1972.

Downs, Anthony. *Inside Bureaucracy*. Boston, Mass.: Little, Brown and Company, 1967.

Fisher, Gene H. *Cost Considerations in Systems Analysis*. New York: American Elsevier Publishing Company, 1971.

Levien, Roger E. (ed.) *The Emerging Technology: Instructional Uses of the Computer in Higher Education*. New York: McGraw-Hill Book Company, 1972.

Marschak, Thomas A., Thomas K. Glennan, Jr., and Robert Summers. *Strategy for R&D*. New York: Springer-Verlag New York, Inc., 1967.

McKean, Roland N. *Efficiency in Government Through Systems Analysis: With Emphasis on Water Resource Development*. New York: John Wiley & Sons, Inc., 1958.

Newhouse, Joseph P. and Arthur J. Alexander. *An Economic Analysis of Public Library Services*. Lexington, Mass.: Lexington Books, D.C. Heath and Company, 1972.

Novick, David (ed.). *Program Budgeting: Program Analysis and the Federal Budget*. Cambridge, Mass.: Harvard University Press, 1965.

Novick, David (ed.). *Current Practice in Program Budgeting (PPBS): Analysis and Case Studies Covering Government and Business*. New York: Crane, Russak and Company, Inc., 1973.

Park, Rolla Edward. *The Role of Analysis in Regulatory Decisionmaking: The Case of Cable Television*. Lexington, Mass.: Lexington Books, D.C. Heath and Company, 1973.

Quade, Edward S., and Wayne I. Boucher. *Systems Analysis and Policy Planning: Applications in Defense*. New York: American Elsevier Publishing Company, 1968.

Turn, Rein. *Computers in the 1980's*. New York: Columbia University Press, 1974.

Williams, John D. *The Compleat Strategyst: Being a Primer on the Theory of Games of Strategy*. New York: McGraw-Hill Book Company, 1966 (rev. ed.).

About the Authors

John G. Wirt is a member of the research staff at The Rand Corporation; he has also served as a budget examiner for the U.S. Bureau of the Budget and as a systems analyst for Sylvania Electronic Defense Laboratories. He received the B.S. in electrical engineering from the University of Minnesota and the M.S. in electrical engineering, and the Ph.D. in engineering and economic systems from Stanford University.

Arnold J. Lieberman is Executive Administrator for Academic Programs for the East-West Center in Honolulu, Hawaii. He has also served as Assistant Dean and Director of Admissions of the Graduate School of Industrial Administration at Carnegie-Mellon University, and as a Rand Corporation Consultant to the Department of Health, Education, and Welfare and to the U.S. Air Force. He received the B.S. in industrial management and the M.S. in industrial administration from Carnegie-Mellon University and the Ph.D. in organizational behavior from Stanford University. He has contributed articles to *The Quarterly Journal of Economics* and *The Journal of Conflict Resolution,* and to *Technological Change: Its Conception and Measurement,* edited by L. Lave (Prentice-Hall, 1966) and *Oligopoly,* edited by Roger Sherman (Lexington Books, 1972).

Roger E. Levien, on leave from his position as Director of Washington Domestic Programs for The Rand Corporation in Washington, D.C., is Executive Editor of the State-of-the-Art Survey Project at the International Institute for Applied Systems Analysis in Laxenburg, Austria. He received the B.S. Engineering from Swarthmore College and the M.S. and Ph.D. in applied mathematics from Harvard University. On the staff of The Rand Corporation since 1956, Dr. Levien has also served as Adjunct Professor of System Sciences at the University of California at Los Angeles since 1970. He is the author of *The Emerging Technology* (McGraw-Hill, 1972) and has contributed articles to *ACM Communications* and *IEEE Transactions on Education.*

DATE DUE

GAYLORD   PRINTED IN U.S.A.